INNER CITY TESTAMENT

COMMUNITY SERIES

Uniform with this Volume

JOHN VINCENT
A LIFESTYLE OF SHARING
The History and Ethos of the Ashram Community
£10

CHRISTIAN COMMUNITIES
Edited by John Vincent
Stories of Eleven Communities, told by themselves
£10

Other volumes in preparation

Copies available from
ASHRAM PRESS
7 College Court, Sheffield S4 7FN; Tel 0114 2436688
Price £10.00 p&p £1.50
Cheques to Ashram Press.

INNER CITY TESTAMENT

Changing the World from the Bottom

JOHN & GRACE

VINCENT

SHEFFIELD

ASHRAM PRESS

INNER CITY TESTAMENT

First published in Great Britain in 2017

Ashram Press

7 College Court

Sheffield S4 7FN

Any Royalties are donated to Ashram Press, which is a not-for-profit imprint of Ashram Community Trust. Registered Charitable Company No.1099164

ISBN : 978-0-9559073-6-4

Phototypeset by Phillippa Thompson

Printed by City Print Services, Atlas Street, Sheffield

CONTENTS

ILLUSTRATIONS

FRONT COVER

John with David Blunkett, 170 Abbeyfield Road, 2010
John and Grace, Oil Painting Portrait by Nick Oldfield, 2016.
Councillors Jackie Drayton and Ibrar Hussein at Grace's Burngreave Distinguished Service Award, 2007
Councillor Jackie Drayton as Lord Mayor, with John as her Chaplain, 2006.
John with Nirmal Fernando and other Multi-Faith Chapel and Library friends on Ellesmere Green, 2008.

BACK COVER

John and Grace at Burngreave Ashram Free Meal, 2017
Ashram Community banner on Anti-Apartheid Demonstration, 1996.
Grace and John with John Howell, High Court, London, 1986.
John with Sheffield PhD graduates Debbie Herring and Steven Heath, 2004.
John with Burngreave New Deal for Communities, 2008.
Grace and John with Chris, Faith and James outside 239 Abbeyfield Road, 1989.

INSIDE PAGES

ACKNOWLEDGEMENTS

We want to thank all those whose names and activities we record. It has been a marvellous privilege to share bits of our lives with them, and bits of their lives with our own.

Especially we thank our family, particularly Faith, who gave it a critical read-through. Three Friends and Colleagues since the 1970's have read and commented helpfully on what we have written – Margaret Mackley (UTU and Ashram), Ian Duffield (UTU) and Ian Lucraft (SICEM).

And we thank Phillippa Thompson who computerised every word of our straggly handwriting. And finally, Ashram Community for receiving this gift into their series. Phillippa's constant plea for a Chapter on "Why", backed up by Faith and James, is met in Chapter 16.

Grateful acknowledgement is also made to *The Guardian*, the *Sheffield Telegraph* and the *Methodist Recorder,* for publishing John's writings over the years, of which fragments are here. and to *The Guardian* for Alice McGregor's Obituary on page 85.

We love reading the life stories of people we have known, and hope that our effort will encourage other contemporaries to write theirs.

During the completion of our book, Grace passed away on 25 May 2017. Reflections of this are in the last two chapters. Otherwise the book remains as we wrote it together.

JOHN & GRACE VINCENT

7 College Court
Sheffield S4 7FN
May 2017

1

INNER CITY TESTAMENT

John and Grace

Testament is an evocative word. The Old Testament is our title for the whole great long history of God's ancient people, the Jews. The New Testament is the records about Jesus and his first Disciples. The novelist Vera Brittain revels in it – Testaments of Youth, Friendship, and Experience.

A Testament, though, is a serious kind of book, one that records facts, places, dates, people, happenings, and occasionally dramatic, amusing or typical cameo stories. It always contains some things that could have been better missed out. But Testament is just what this person or couple or group have chosen to set down. They cannot deny it, it just happened some way, like this – always it's warts and all, but also not missing the many-splendoured thing. But not always explaining things, you'd have to say. It's a Testament to things that happened, not necessarily an Apologia justifying all of them.

INNER CITY

Our Testament comes from the Inner City. It tells how we got here, what we did here, what we learnt here, what we planted here, and what we landed ourselves with here. We still live within a hundred yards of our two previous houses. It's a somewhat long incarnation. With only occasional, brief ascensions.

Inner City may be strange to you. There is much on it here. In the first chapter of my *Into The City*, I give a taste of how it first felt to move here – cold, unwelcoming, restricting, I called it.

9

But the people who are here today feel remarkably like those we found in 1970 when we arrived. Our list was.

Survivors who did not do well and move out, single parent families, non-coping families, students, ex-students, drop outs, people in part-time jobs, men and women running do-it-yourself crafts and industries, recent immigrants from the non industrialised countries, refugees.

It's still on our streets, much the same. The inner city does not change much. Though the numbers of the last two groups have greatly increased.

With my knowledge of the situation in first century Galilee and its importance to Jesus' life and work, I realised that this situation that we faced and still face is remarkably like the one that Jesus both faced in his native environment and chose to remain in, choose his disciples out of, and get his parables from, and whose political and community life he would choose as the place within which he would claim that what he called "God's Kingdom" was now actually present here on earth. So how could we realise that for our Galilee, our inner city? That became our calling.

So this is our Testament to our attempts to live as if all this was happening and also actually to make happen a few bits of it!

Our Testament is to a strange ongoing Reality – and coming from our equally strange context in the inner city today.

Reference
John J Vincent, *Into The City*. London: Epworth Press, 1982, p 16

2

CHILDHOOD IN MANCHESTER

John

My parents, David Vincent and Ethel Beatrice Gadd, were married in Edenbridge, Kent on 5th April 1926. David was a manager with Thoroughgood, a retail provisions firm. Ethel had previously worked at Sainsbury's in Tunbridge Wells, to which David had come as a relief manager in 1923. David's job was to open new shops. He was in Nottingham, where my older brother Gordon was born, in 1927, in Sunderland, in 1929 for my birth and then in Urmston for the birth of Peter in 1933.

My Father died in 1976. When I was around eight, Dad took me to Stradbroke in Suffolk (where he later gave two bells in memory of two brothers who died in 1914-18), and I recall walking across a field in Campse Ash, in which there was an empty cottage. He and his six brothers had slept in one bedroom. The surname Vincent is, of course, Latin or Gallic, and probably our ancestors were part of the Norman invasion of 1066. Our branch came through a Suffolk peasant line.

My mother lived to 109 and died in 2000, after being with us in our home from 1986. She had kept a Journal, which our daughter Faith worked at, and published in 2008 in a volume of recollections and pictures – *The Memoirs of Ethel Beatrice Vincent 1891-2000*.

Mother records my arrival as follows in her Memoirs:

"John arrived (after I had made 24 mince pies in the morning) safely on 29 Dec 1929 at Roker, Sunderland. A very wintery day, lots of snow everywhere, only the main roads were useable. Both the doctor and the nurse had to walk quite a distance, but I had a dear friend with me. She was splendid and a great comfort. We had another dear little son!" (pp 46-7).

EARLY YEARS

From April 1933, Dad was working in York and we lived in Haxby. In January 1935, I spent a month at Haxby Primary School, but then in February we all moved to a house in Hale, Cheshire, very near Stamford Park Primary and Junior School, which we attended.

Dad had finally got tired of being an itinerant shop manager, and resigned from Thoroughgoods, and opened his own business at 49 Railway Street, Altrincham. It was "Provisions Only" – a miniature J.Sainsbury's. In 1938, he opened a second shop in Northwich, though it had to close in 1942. I worked on Saturdays in one or other of the shops, and became adept at carving hams, of which we would cook 20 or 30 a week in the cellar of the Altrincham shop.

Peter's chapter in the EBV Memoirs tells how he developed the business from one to nine branches in Altrincham (2) Sale, Sale Moor, Stretford, Timperley, Macclesfield, Wilmslow and Whiston. The last branch to close in 1992 was the first. It had been a "niche market", but declined, as Peter says, with the rise of supermarkets and the decline of the main street, and changes in shopping habits. But it was great while it lasted, with Gordon's farm at Charlesworth supplying "Honey Brown Farm Eggs". It was all going well, when Dad died in 1976.

After war began in September 1939, our lives changed dramatically. Dad's provision merchant business at 49 Railway Street, Altrincham, lost most of its specialist sales items immediately, and he was compelled to take groceries as well, to keep his "registered customers", whose coupons we would zealously count on the dining room table, all the family together.

HOME LIFE

Another family event was hand bell ringing. We formed a team able to ring "Caters" (10 bells), and each of us became adept at ringing our pair of hand bells in the right order – Dad, 1-2, Gordon, 3-4, John, 5-6, Peter, 7-8, and Mother 9-10. The family practices at home were riotous, occasionally tearful, occasions. But they led to performances in halls and churches around the area which made us all glow with pride.

It was a happy childhood, and I totally concur with my brother Gordon's chapter on "Childhood and Family Life" in the EBV Memoirs. I quote one paragraph.

"The pinnacle of Mother's week, now she had a maid, was organizing Sunday Lunch in the dining room. Always three courses, the best silver – yes, silver that had to be cleaned in those days, was laid out, in front of her boys, who had been washed and in their "Sunday Best" ready for departure at 2.15pm prompt to Sunday School. This was a mammoth task, getting this to her high standards. We had probably been helping father in the morning in our "roughs", anything from gardening to recreosoting pagodas. In our hectic life of today all this may appear very pedestrian, but to mother, the home and the way it was run was of prime importance, just as father judged success in business terms." (p.97)

Mother was artistic and had beautiful handwriting, and taught me piano. Together, we went to plays at the Garrick, Altrincham, and to Donald Wolfit's Shakespeare Company and to Ballet at the Palace and the Opera House in Manchester – all this in the later war years, 1943-45, and 1945- 49. Mother and I seemed to be "on the same wavelength", and we instinctively understood each other.

MANCHESTER GRAMMAR SCHOOL

By dint of considerable sacrifice, our parents managed to send all three boys to Sale High School and Manchester Grammar School. Both Gordon and Peter left MGS after School Certificate age 16, when Gordon went into agriculture, and Peter joined Dad in the family business. I was always the rather weaker and frailer of the three of us, and the family supported me to stay at school till 18, when I went into the army. Much later, Gordon confided that keeping me at MGS for two and a half extra years was a real drain on the family finances. In 1944 Father cashed in his "Hearts of Oak" Benefit Society insurance to keep the school bills paid, though they were related to parents' income.

Peter was always a great self-starter and totally committed supporter of his own originality and genius. Dad always said the other two brothers would end up asking Peter for a loan! (Actually, we

14

didn't!). Gordon and I repeated these and many other happy memories at our younger brother Peter's Funeral at the old Bowdon Parish Church, which we attended as children, on 19th March 2013. I spoke at Peter's widow, Margaret's funeral at Bowdon on 1st April 2014, and conducted Gordon's, on 19th May 2014 in Bridlington, where his widow Audrey still lives.

The daily round trip to Manchester Grammar School was a real fact of life, I would take the tram along Upper Brook Street or the bus along Oxford Road, get off at Oxford Road Station, but then walk up to Central Library, where I could sit and read – or occasionally at John Rylands Library in Deansgate. Quite often, I went into the Portico Gallery on Lower Mosley Street, and was enthralled by the Pre-Raphaelites there – Holman Hunt, Ford Madox Ford, and Dante Gabriel Rosetti.

Immediately post-war, Britain was sparse in every way. The Lyons Corner Café in Albert Square would have pieces of bread or toast, plus margarine and jam – and of course cups of tea. But the sparseness said that you must create meaning and value within yourself. This meant for me art and reading. For Higher School Certificate I did Economics "Subsid" and Art, English, and History

I was in History Sixth, at Manchester Grammar with Walter Schwarz (journalist), Peter Dawson and Michael Henshall (Anglican clergy) and Kenneth Richardson (Teacher, Methodist Local Preacher). They were good days. The High Master, Dr. Eric James, was friendly and supportive. He got me to read the lesson in Assembly on many occasions, and would discuss the passage with me. He did a lesson weekly of "RE", and gave us lectures on Ephesians and Plato. He encouraged the SCM/IVF Group which I started and ran for 2 years. Finally, he got me in January 1948 to the major SCM Congress in Westminster. Two memories of speakers remain. One is of the brilliance of Reinhold Neibuhr. But, even more I recall the passion for the poor of Father St. John B Groser. More significant was that, together with another student, I took off for two nights which we spent in the Old Kent Road, talking to street sleepers and people running soup kitchens. I knew that I had to become an inner city minister. But I told no-one.

HALE METHODIST CHURCH

Hale Methodist Church was the decisive seed-bed for my Christian Faith from age 5 to age 20. I would name three factors in the Christianity it represented which were formative for me. I wrote them down for their 1997 Centenary Booklet, and reprinted them in *Methodism Unbound* (2015)

"First, the sheer commitment, warmth, friendliness and openness of everyone. It was a loving, caring fellowship of warm, sincere people, who gave themselves endlessly to others, especially those growing up in their midst. Above all was Tony Stocks, who opened his home to myself and two or three others, and who gently brought me into taking part in meetings and studying the Christian truths and ways."

"Second, the broad, accepting, liberal, tolerant, expectant, intellectual and spiritual attitudes of the place. Sermons were heard and discussed, ideas were welcomed, and discussion was expected. And I was listened to, long before I had anything to say! I started preaching at 15 and candidated for the ministry at 19, but it seemed natural to do so in the context of the stimulation and support that was all around. And I got confidence through the many amateur dramatic productions in which I took part, at church and elsewhere."

"Third, the centrality of Jesus, and endless fascination with the lifestyle of Jesus. I like to think that I offered for the ministry because it was an easy way to be paid full time for doing what I really wanted to do – be a full time disciple of Jesus. But that discipleship to Jesus was conceived by me as something worth doing was surely not due to my own insight but to the ethos of Jesus and discipleship which I imbibed from Hale Methodist Church."

TEENAGE YEARS

At fourteen, I got together the basics of the preacher's trade – a Methodist Hymn Book from Tony Stocks, a Revised Version Bible from my parents, plus Cruden's Concordance and Roget's Thesaurus – still basics on my desk today.

At fifteen, I discovered other helps. Hartley Victoria College was cycling distance away at Fallowfield. There, the Principal, Rev. John T. Wilkinson, and the Theology Tutor, Dr. Percy Scott, gave me time and counsel, and much encouragement. Percy had a D.Theol. from Marburg, this stuck in my mind. Later in 1966, he handed over his annual US lecture itinerary to me, which got me into Seminaries and needed publications to have with me.

Another decisive influence was that, perhaps because of shyness (shy people need a role to play!), I became an amateur actor. Between 1943 and 1950, I was a member of several Amateur Dramatic Societies – Hale St. David's, Hale Congregational, Manchester Independent Theatre Guild and (with myself as producer) Hale Methodist. At MGS, I played in Shaw's *St Joan* and Shakespeare's *Julius Caesar*.

MILITARY SERVICE

Military Service started in February 1948, and I joined the Royal Army Medical Corps. After 3 months I was posted to Waringfield Military Hospital in Moira. County Down, N.I. By now, only the Methodist Ministry was in my sights. I led weekly Sunday Fellowship in the Camp Theatre, where I also produced a Christmas 1949 play, *A Christmas Carol*. In September 1949 I sent in the application form for Methodist ministry. It asked what kind of ministry I was offering for – I wrote "City Missions".

I finished military service as Chief Clerk – and a Sergeant – at Waringfield, and returned in January 1950. Thinking that I needed practical experience as a working labourer, I spent eight months in a small firm making concrete – Concrete Industries Altrincham, at Broadheath. Then in June I was accepted for the Ministry at the 1950 Methodist Conference.

3

CHILDHOOD IN INDIA

Grace

I was born on 12th April 1934 in an American hospital in Kodikanal in South India. My early years, until the age of 14, were spent in South India. I was living there because my Dad was an Irish Methodist missionary. This time in my life has many lovely and striking memories for me. The earliest reference to me was in a letter from my mother to a friend dated 27 June 1934.

"Yes! It is quite a joy having a baby to look after and sometimes my husband can scarcely believe that this wee mite is really ours. She has been doing very well and gaining weight steadily".

The whole missionary tradition was in a very colonial context. We lived in a lovely big bungalow with many servants! Earlier missionaries had built several enormous cathedral-like churches, utterly inappropriate for the small towns they were in, but drawing thousands of worshippers on a Sunday.

Dad used to go on tour to small remote isolated villages in a bandy cart pulled by bullocks. He conducted services, baptisms and weddings and he slept in a tent, he and the equipment cared for by servants. We sometimes went too. I also spoke the Telegu language, better when very young.

It is easy to be critical of the whole colonial style, but in fact Dad was much loved and sought after. The servants greatly valued their jobs and our family were loved and respected.

Then when I was only five years old, I was amazingly sent to a boarding school called Hebron in Coonoor, 3 days journey to the South West, high among the tea bushes. It was run by Australians and New Zealanders and was the only way to get an education in English. And I loved it.

TEENS AND TWENTIES

In 1948 aged fourteen, my mother brought me and my two brothers, Frederick and Gorman, back to Northern Ireland for further education. I have vivid memories of travelling home on a troop ship with a huge number of troops and just a few other civilians. We came through the Suez Canal and the Mediterranean.

My father came back to Ireland from India in 1950, and served as a Methodist Minister in Cork, Newtownards, Lurgan and Bangor where he retired in 1968. Mother died in 1996, and Father in 1997. In 1999 I got together a booklet, *Wilfred and Dora Stafford*, with their own recollections plus articles by people who knew and loved them. Additionally the book included many wonderful photographs of their lives. I wrote:

"It was a magic childhood really, with deeply committed and loving parents, whose giving of themselves shaped many lives and is still remembered in India"

In Ulster, I went to Methodist College Belfast, where I became Head Girl of the Boarding department. Then I had four years across the road in Queen's University studying English, which I later used to teach English as a Second Language in Sheffield.

Thinking I might become a Personnel Manager, I spent a year in Manchester to get a Diploma in Personnel Management. I got involved in the Student Christian Movement and in the Campaign for Nuclear Disarmament.

JOHN AND I MEET

On Saturday the 24th February 1958, having nothing better to do, I went to an SCM Retreat in Mottram. It was led by John Vincent!

In 1958, John and I spent most Saturdays together organizing Campaign for Nuclear Disarmament demonstrations in Wythenshawe shopping centres. In April I joined John for the Order of Christian

Witness Campaign he led in Hazel Grove. In June and July, John was in Basel working on his Doctorate – which he finally got in May 1960.

And on 4th December 1958 we were married in Lurgan, Northern Ireland, where dad was the Minister, at Queen's Street Methodist Church. We returned to live at John's little council house Manse at Rodborough Road, Wythenshawe, and started our ministry.

In 2008, my brother Gorman, his wife Sue and I went back to India for an amazing visit to all the places we had lived. Gorman had been only 2 years old when we left but I was 14. Everywhere we went – Karim Nagar, Medak, Hyderabad and then the Nilgiri Hills in the South – seemed very little changed. And we met folk who remembered Mum and Dad and even found a loved photo of my Dad in the Medak vestry, looking very young in it.

Gorman and Sue are in Cheltenham, where Sue was a teacher, and Gorman, Headmaster of Secondary Schools. My other brother, Frederick, is only four years younger than myself. He now lives in Notting Hill, where Derick is an Architect and his wife Sheila a teacher.

4

FINDING A WAY

John

From whence does one find one's way?

From whence have come things in myself which I do either automatically or out of some kind of conviction? From my early years, my father as a provision merchant gave the instruction "Never sell anything to anyone else that you would not eat yourself." Which I think of often today when dishing up free meals. From Amateur Theatricals, I got a lasting love of performance, for words, for hyperbole, for playing a part. From Tony Stocks who first taught me by example how to create and sustain a group of lads by a combination of letting us play with the family's enormous train set to lending us Christian books, I got things which I practice today.

From Percy Scott at Hartley Victoria College who took me in as a 15 year old, and lent me books to read and opened up Christian Scholarship to me; I learned to look around for those from whom I might learn. "Find the Greathearts, and learn from them, John", he told me. "Start with Bill Gowland". I did.

It was the death of W.R. Maltby in 1951 that first made me determined to go and visit and learn from those I might see as exemplars or masters. This took me to go to Donald Soper, George MacLeod, Oscar Cullmann, Karl Barth, T.W. Manson, Eduard Schweizer, and John Tinsley – the last three writers on my Discipleship preoccupation. All had special gifts and expertise which I wanted, or had worked at things for which I felt an instinctive call, which needed to be tested by others who seemed to have similar calls – to see what they had done with their calls. Brian O' Gorman, who had also gone into Methodist ministry from Hale, became a friend and affirmer, too – and many others at particular points in my life.

They were all people of passion who put their passions into practice by creating projects. Such would be my way.

NEWENT

On 1st September 1950 I arrived in Newent, Gloucestershire, sent as a Pre-collegiate Probationer Methodist Minister. I had "digs" with a delightful farming couple, Andrew and Kate Ford. They felt I looked undernourished, so generously fed me up.

Newent was a delight. Dad gave me an ancient, very heavy bicycle, and I spent most days cycling around one or other of my five small country chapels – at Newent, Redmarley, Upleadon, Kent's Green and Pendock. I had a brilliant, generous Superintendent Minister, Thomas Martin, who looked after his "young colleague" with great insight. He even secretly came over to my side of the (Ledbury) Circuit, and got local people in Pool Hill to labour with him to open a derelict chapel – to which he then introduced their young minister in Easter 1951.

RICHMOND COLLEGE

In early September 1951, Dad and Mum motored down to Richmond, Surrey and proudly installed me as the first member in their families' histories to get to a University, even if it was only a Methodist Ministerial Training College. The three years there were rather intense, with great rivalry between students. We had a Reunion in 2001, and were amazed how little we had changed! But we all had achieved bits of significant or at least faithful ministry.

My most unexpected bonus was that as soon as I arrived at Richmond College in September 1951, I joined Douglas Bibb and other Kingsway Hall and Order of Christian Witness friends in keeping Donald Soper's 3pm Hyde Park Sunday open air Meeting going while he was in Australia. So after a few weeks, I became the sole occupant of Donald's stand, and spoke there for an hour each week from October to December. On my third occasion, a regular highly verbal member of the crowd found me addressing 5 or 6 people and shouted "Shall we get a crowd?" "Yes please", I replied in desperation. The questioner immediately launched into a tirade –

"You're not Donald Soper. So where is the old buffer?" The crowd soon gathered.

At Richmond we spread our wings as we could. I was college Librarian and edited the magazine *The Old Chariot*. I led the Hyde Park Saturday evening Open Air Mission Band, produced and directed W.B. Yeats' *Land of Heart's Desire*, and was a member of the College Debating Team with David Mason and Geoff Ainger, much respected seniors to myself. Also on the 15th October 1953, I made my first entry in the *Methodist Recorder*, with a letter objecting to a front page article urging "We Must Stay in Tune with America". The 26 of us who signed it became known as "the 26" and Prof Bertram Clogg always referred to people with a twinkle in his eye as "One of the twenty six".

Also in September 1953, I visited Leslie Hunter, Bishop of Sheffield, to see if I could be an Anglican Ordinand as well. It led nowhere, though Donald supported it.

My dominant memory of Richmond College and the London BD course was for the first time actually ploughing through the Old Testament, including a year studying the Hebrew text. I learned enough of the appalling records of violence, lust, deception, double-dealing and special pleading contained there, to conclude a permanent feeling that Christianity was better founded elsewhere.

So could Christianity be founded solely on Jesus? I had wanted to be a disciple of Jesus, who obviously valued the Old Testament. But how much did I need to carry it with me?

I developed the conviction that we, or I at least, had to work at an understanding of Jesus, sufficiently autonomous and significant that it could be lived out and commended to others today. With the help of Harold Roberts, the Richmond Principal, I got a $500 scholarship to be at Drew Theological Seminary, Madison, NJ, for the Year, 1954-55. With the help of a Fulbright grant, I sailed on the Queen Elizabeth liner and back on the Queen Mary.

DREW AND BASEL

America was in the grip of McCarthyism. They sent me a booklet, *Is There a Pink Fringe in the Methodist Church?* I thought that would be a great idea, but saw little evidence of it. At Easter

1955, I went by Greyhound bus through Richmond, Virginia to Nashville, Tennessee. For a decade, Roger Ortmayer got me to write articles for the Methodist Student magazine *Motive*. In Nashville he had me speak at a couple of rallies of the National Association for the Advancement of Coloured People. And at Drew, I started a long association with Black Methodists in Newark, NJ, which blossomed into the Urban Theology Unit, North America, founded with Geoff Curtiss in the Red House, opposite Newark Cathedral, later in 1979.

The Drew course was towards their STM – Sacrae Theologicae Magister, Master of Sacred Theology. Martin Luther named it as his qualification at the top of his Ninety Nine Theses in 1517.

I spent the whole year writing papers on Discipleship, for the various courses and seminars I attended, led by leading scholars – Carl Michalson, Bernhard Anderson, Howard Clark Kee, William R. Farmer, Henry J. Cadbury, Paul Lehmann, Franz Hildebrandt. I refused to read Dietrich Bonheoffer's *Cost of Discipleship*, just published in 1948, so that I would work at the New Testament material without any preconceptions. In March 1955 Professor Oscar Cullmann came and lectured at Drew. As I did with every scholar I met, I tried to persuade him of my conviction that Christianity could be based solely on – first Jesus, and then second, Discipleship, as in the Jesus of the Gospels, rather than Belief, as developed by Paul.

Cullmann persuaded Drew to give me $600 to go to Basel in Switzerland for a year to start a Doctorate. So I arrived in September 1955 and lived in his Theologisches Alumneum at 17 Hebelstrasse, for a year of study and writing. In Basel, of course, was also Karl Barth, and his fortnightly English Speaking Colloquium held in the Bruderholz Cafe was a real boon, alongside Barth's many American Students, among whom I got to know and value John Godsey, Shirley Guthrie, John Deschner, and Ted Runyon (at Göttingen). David Bosch and Andre duToit from South Africa were fellow New Testament students studying with Cullmann, plus John Miller of USA.

In the summer of 1956, I returned to Hale, where Mum and Dad still lived. The Methodist Conference was in Leeds, and my parents came with me to the Centenary Methodist Church in York, where I was ordained as a Methodist Minister in July, having completed my six years of Probation. Donald Soper preached, and I got the sermon published in the *Epworth Review* from a tape of it.

MANCHESTER MISSION

I had persuaded the dour Scots Superintendent of the Manchester and Salford Mission, James Morrison Neilson, to let me go as a minister to two churches in the sprawling new housing estate of Wythenshawe. The place was just two miles away from where my parents were living – and also 2 miles from Hale Barns, where my younger brother Peter and his new wife Margaret lived. But the journey from Hale to Baguley was a journey between two very different worlds. It was my first experiment with trying to live in irreconcilable worlds, which became a vital part of my life thereafter.

For the years 1957-1960, I persuaded the Manchester Mission to let me go back to Basel for six weeks each May – June, to complete my studies. A Baguley Hall member, Nora Carter, generously offered to type out my dissertation. Then in June 1960, I was awarded the Doctorate in Theology *insigni cum laude* after a 3-hour 'Doctor Prüfung' with Oscar Cullmann, Karl Barth, Bo Reicke and Julius Schweitzer as my examiners. My dissertation set out the grounds for my Jesus-centred Discipleship convictions, and was called "Disciple and Lord: the Historical and Theological Significance of Discipleship in the Synoptic Gospels." I published the printed version in 1975. Karl Barth invited me to his home for an hour's discussion on my thesis. The theology he vigorously opposed – 'Schrecklich' (terrible!) he called it. But at the end, when asked about what I should do, he replied; "Mr. Vincent, it is right for you. You have to do what you have to do – as I did."

Every year from 1950 to 1960 I spent a week or two of my holidays in August and at Easter at the campaigns of Donald Soper and the Order of Christian Witness. These brought up to 350 young adults into key cities for street preaching, visiting, debating and work with young people, with every day a memorable Worship and Community hour led by Donald Soper. A whole generation of us were formed by this – not least contemporaries and supporters of myself like Harry Morton and David Mason – the three of us joining smaller campaigns together.

TILL THIRTY

Plato advised giving oneself wholly to study until the age of thirty. George MacLeod counselled a celibate ministry until thirty.

26

Harry Morton wrote wondering whether he should ever ask a woman to share the kind of ministry he felt called to. But at 24 and 28, Grace and I met, got married, and started our joint ministry, the theme of the next chapter, and the rest of this book.

I belonged to a group of young ministers, all busy 'Finding our Way'. We taught each other, and learned from each other. I recall in the late 1950's, Dick Jones appearing at my door in Wythenshawe and saying, "John, you run a newspaper. Show me how it's done." Or a few years later, we had a group of young ministers on housing estates, and went for a day to Bill Davies in Langley, Middleton. Or when I came to Rochdale, one of my first calls was to W.H. Vanstone, in Kirkholt – to learn how to be a theologian within an urban ministry.

I recall complaining to George MacLeod that I was exhausted by six days morn til night ministry in Rochdale, so that I often had to write on Saturdays. He replied; "What you write on the Saturday is richer because you have done the ministry all week".

5

HOUSING ESTATE

Grace

After our marriage on 4th December 1958, I joined John in the council house which served as a manse, 4 Rodborough Road, Newall Green, Wythenshawe.

I was able to get some part time teaching of English, at The College of Catering in Rusholme. Then I did 2 years teaching at Poundswick Secondary School in Woodhouse Park just 10 minutes walk away. .

Our life together revolved around John's two churches. The first, Baguley Hall, was a large gymnasium-like dual purpose building in the heart of the estate.

John's smaller church was Higher Baguley Methodist Chapel, an old country Chapel just off the estate. Here I led a youth group, and we took groups out for weekends to John's parents' home at Mere Hayes, near Lymm, with Arthur Francis and others as key members.

BAGULEY HALL METHODIST CHURCH

John was really pleased with his friends and supporters in both churches – both of which were happy, committed and imaginative communities. The Whit walk procession brought out large crowds. In spring 1958, John produced and acted in Christopher Fry's *A Sleep of Prisoners*, with Brian Todd, Bill Slack, and Kenneth Smith as his co-stars. It was a memorable production, which was taken around local halls and churches. John started a Men's Society, which had 30 members. This group discussed current local and political issues.

When asked to write something for a Baguley Hall Anniversary Booklet in 2000, John wrote

"Baguley days were for me days of great happiness and fulfilment. I had never wanted to be anything else but a Methodist Minister, and here I was at 26 actually doing it, surrounded by some amazing and courageous people, who would listen, but then take up what I had said."

"Typical was my colleagueship with Brian Todd in the *Baguley Methodist News*, which we published every month for five years. We felt we had failed if we did not get into the *Manchester Evening News* every month or two. And every month we commented on local community, national and (less so!) church events."

"The mid fifties to early sixties in Baguley Hall were, I fancy, its heyday. We (not I) managed to catch the imagination and commitment of ex-servicemen by then in their forties, with growing families. We boasted at one time as many males as females in the membership, an unusual phenomenon then as now. Membership went up from around 50 in 1956 to around 150 in 1962. We had numbers and the leaders to make an impact, and in our own way, I think we did."

In 1960, Donald Soper came to Baguley Hall to speak for John at a meeting. We discovered that 'Sergeant Bilko' was on BBC TV at 8.30pm. "Can we get back in time?", asked Donald. We did!

Our first son Christopher John was born in St Mary's Hospital, Oxford Road, on 29 March 1961. He was for us a real 'Christ-bearer' – hence 'Christopher'. We were very busy with CND, and Chris got the dedication in *Christ in a Nuclear World*.

CAMPAIGN FOR NUCLEAR DISARMAMENT

In CND, we got a 10,000 signature petition against nuclear weapons raised through Wythenshawe open air meetings in estate shopping centres. In May 1962, John spoke at the Free Trade Hall in Manchester, with Bertrand Russell, John Collins and Joseph Rotblat. He raised a record collection of £2000. Also at a Free Trade Hall CND Rally in February 1962, John's first book, *Christ in a Nuclear World* was launched, and we sold 500 copies. The same year, we joined the CND Aldermaston March, walking with Christopher in his pushchair.

Christ in a Nuclear World had been read and commented on by Donald Soper, who wrote to 'cordially commend' the book. George MacLeod wrote the Foreword which ended: "That John Vincent speaks so concisely and so clearly to the modern mind is due to his constant involvement with Mission to the Ordinary Man in Manchester today. His reputation in that city is rapidly becoming national in its impact." John Robinson, then Bishop of Woolwich, wrote "The best book so far on the distinctively Christian responsibility in this terrible field. It comes from a first-class young New Testament Scholar, who is technically informed and politically engaged."

John was also a member of the British Council of Churches Commission, which produced the report *The British Nuclear Deterrent* (1963), to which John wrote an alternative view in *Christian Nuclear Perspective* (1964), with parts appearing first in *Frontier* and *The British Weekly*. The Methodist Conference adopted a Unilateralist resolution in July 1963, and John joined a 3-day Lambeth Palace group of Bishops and theologians called by Archbishop Michael Ramsey in December 1963.

TRAVELS

In May 1962, John was in Washington DC, for the US Fellowship of Reconciliation and in July 1963 in Moscow at a Disarmament and Peace Conference. He recalls a long conversation with John and Diana Collins on the return flight concerning St. Paul's Cathedral. In 1965 he was in Leningrad for a Christian Peace Conference Consultation, with Gordon Rupp, with whom he spent a return overnight in Helsinki, marked by typical Rupp conviviality and wit, and later in Budapest, Prague and Berlin. He also did lectures on Gospel studies at the Oxford Congresses on the New Testament, 1957, 1961 and 1965. From 1962 to 2002, he was eight times a member of the Oxford Institute of Methodist Theological Studies, which meets five yearly.

In spring 1962, John's varied activities produced invitations from British SCM to be their Study Secretary, from Candler School of Theology at Emory, Atlanta to be a New Testament Associate Professor, and from the BBC to join the Religious Broadcasting Staff.

But we were set for going to the Methodist Mission Hall in Rochdale. And John in June/July was in Moscow for a World Congress on General Disarmament and Peace, in the Kremlin. So life was already overloaded, in terms of John's urban mission vocation, let alone his New Testament one. I shared whenever I could, including being a member of the CND North West Executive. I also became the Treasurer for a Medical Aid for Vietnam Fund we started in 1960.

6

CITY CENTRE

Grace

We moved to Rochdale in September 1962, when Christopher was 18 months old.

Our second child, Helen Faith, was born on 5th April 1964, in Oldham General Hospital. George MacLeod was with us and baptised Faith on 3rd May 1964, which John records in his dedication to George of his book *Christ and Methodism* in 1965.

Our third child, James Stafford was born on 8th October 1966 and, was baptised by my father on 22 January 1967, as the dedication to *Secular Christ* says.

At Rochdale, we first lived in the old manse at 47 Falinge Road, opposite Falinge Park, and then moved in 1966 to a larger house with a big garden at 669 Oldham Road.

Daily life began with getting the children off to school. Methodist ministerial salaries were never adequate. So, I got part time work teaching in a local school, and also earned money by spending each June marking School Certificate English exam papers.

CHAMPNESS HALL

John left the house at 8.45 and spent each morning down at Rochdale Methodist Mission, which was at Champness Hall, Drake Street, servicing meetings or organisations.

In 1963, John produced a Plan, *Ground for Meeting* and raised £20,000 to carry out a total modernisation of the enormous premises. By 1967, we were running a weekly Play Centre, an

International Centre, an Ecumenical Centre, and had altered the whole second floor to create a nightly Youth Club, led by one of our members, Randal Cropper, whom we had sent away to train. My own project was to set up and maintain a Young Wives Club, which ended with 30 members, most of whom came with their children to the Family Worship, which replaced the evening service as the main worship occasion. George MacLeod preached to 250 at a Rededicated Hall on May 18th 1968.

John had a succession of brilliant Wesley Deaconess colleagues – Patricia Sims (1962-3), Kathleen Fountain (1963-4), Vera Allcott (1964-68) and Marjorie James (1968-70). Kathleen later became a Methodist Minister, then was the first woman President of Conference in 1992-3, and finally became Lady Richardson in the House of Lords in 1998. Vera Allcott married Graham Slater and worked with him at the Hartley Victoria College in Manchester.

Marjorie James, later Bonehill was part of Ashram Community from its beginning and in the East End of London and finally in Marple, and remaining part of Ashram until her death in April 2017.

RESIDENTIAL COMMUNITY

In 1966 we created a Residential Community on the second floor, where five young men lived and worked with us. A great colleague in all this was resident warden, Cyril Harman, who spent five happy years with us. Meantime in the Central Hall itself, we redesigned the front creating a sanctuary, which included a huge controversial Byzantine tapestry of Christ by Audrey Tucker. The residential community included long-time friends like Rodney Fielding, Stuart Jordan, David Gamble and Michael Fielding, all of whom became Methodist Ministers. From 1967, John secured the colleagueship of another Methodist minister, Tony Wesson, who was the North West Regional Lay Training Officer and worked with Pauline Webb who had been the National Secretary of Lay Training. Tony lived in Rochdale, creating with us the Mission Team Ministry, which included all eight mission staff and the community members.

In July 1967, John and four younger lay friends called a conference named "Living and Surviving in Methodism Today". The forty five who came decided to stay together and formed an Intentional Community. Looking for a title they found Hendrik Kraemer describing an Ashram as "combining the Indian idea of retreat for the cultivation of the spiritual life with the European idea of settlement for service of the environment." So the name Ashram was chosen and has stuck.

ALTERNATIVE FUTURES

In March and April 1967, Donald Soper wrote some short articles in the *Methodist Recorder* on his four great platforms – sacramentalism, evangelism, socialism and pacifism. These seemed to John to be shielding us from perceiving what we really needed. So in four articles in May 1967 he urged substitutes. The living Lord eating with modern disciples alongside publicans and sinners for sacramentalism; the practice of running play centres and organising community for evangelism; political activism rather than pacifism; and contemporary radical experimentalism and projects rather than socialism.

"Clearly rattled by Vincent's alternative vision" in the words of Donald's biographer Mark Peel (p.225), Donald replied a month later at some length. And David Mason warned John that Donald did not take kindly to comments, much less criticism, and that he should watch his step.

But *The Observer* of 19 March 1967 featured John, also Pauline Webb, in a magazine article on "Saving the Sermon." And a lay Leader from the City Temple in London looking for a successor to Leslie Weatherhead came to hear him twice. Certainly the Rochdale years were hideously busy for John. He was constantly in local, regional and national press and radio, either on CND or local or political questions. *The Rochdale Observer* frequently picked up issues raised in John's monthly newspaper, *Today*. In between it all, he published his key position-taking Theological books, *Christ and Methodism* (1965), *Secular Christ* (1967) and *Here I Stand* (1968), all of which created much controversy and many calls to travel.

He would always try to be back in Rochdale for Sundays, for the morning and evening services. When he gave the week-long daily Rall lectures at Garrett Theological Seminary at Evanston Illinois in March 1969, he travelled to and fro on the Monday and Saturday! The subject was 'The Dynamics of Christ', later popularised in *The Jesus Thing* (an "execrable title", said Dick Jones) in 1973, revised in *Christ in the City* in 2013

In Spring 1969, John received an invitation from J Robert Nelson to fill a semester sabbatical for him and to teach Theology as Visiting Professor, at Boston University, USA. While he was away we found a small house to rent in Manchet Street, Castleton. Daily from there I delivered the children to schools and then taught full time in Oldham. Our youngest, James spent each day with a wonderful Champness Hall couple, Richard and Florrie Kay.

John returned for Christmas, and we opened the first Ashram Community House in King St. South, with our friends Peter Crompton, Chris Blackwell, Gladys Brierley, and Elaine Peace as residents. From February to May, John was teaching with Bill Webber at the New Year Theological Seminary, and trying to get together plans to start the Urban Theology Unit in summer 1970.

MY WORK AS A TEACHER

My teaching in Oldham was English as a Second Language. I had never taught this before, and there were no training courses. So I had to invent it as I went along. And the students were teenagers! It was all incredibly demanding.

My teaching career continued part time for 26 years. When we moved to Sheffield in September 1970, I taught similarly at Byron Wood Middle School. Again I had to create the whole course. In 1985, I was moved to Earl Marshall Secondary School. By this time I had worked out a whole method, and I had a classroom where the students came, when they first arrived in this country. I was able to develop my course into a rich and varied one, also including bits of geography and facts about life in England that they would need. They were with me full time until they seemed ready to cope in the main school.

I retired in 1996. I still meet people I taught who stop me in the street and they are full of happy memories of our time together. Very recently, I met a man who had now had four children who reminded me with delight that I used to take them on picnics and during half-term would continue the classes in our house. I also taught Ibrar Hussein, later our local councillor.

Reference

Mark Peel, *The Last Wesleyan: A Life of Donald Soper* (Lancaster:Scotforth Books 2008)

7

INTENTIONAL COMMUNITY

John

"START-UPS"

Around 1967, I recall Donald Soper saying to me that whatever you were going to do, you should have started by forty. So, around my 40th birthday (29 December 1969), I faced seriously the problem that the special things that I felt it was my calling to secure, or invent or construct, would all have to be done by myself. Each would mean a sort of "creation out of nothing". Each would identify a particular area of concern which I felt to be important. Each would only succeed insofar as they brought others into them, for each of them depended on finding fellow-travellers, or at least others who might not be able to create things, but would join them if someone started them. That meant I had to do "unilateral initiatives."

So I gave myself to "start-ups", with the agonies of finding allies, facing vested interests, and interminable internal questions of mission, legitimacy, credibility, maintenance, and survival which led to years of hard labour!

Urban Theology Unit and Sheffield Inner City Ecumenical Mission (in Chapter 8) are 'start-ups' still continuing. Of the other 4 in this chapter, only Ashram Community continues today. So the only surviving "start-ups" are the three Inner City ones, probably because nobody else wants to be there!

All are "Intentional Communities" – groups with special purposes.

METHODIST RENEWAL GROUP

From the early years of my ministry, I had tried to explain and justify my commitment to my chosen denomination – Methodism.

In May 1960 I was passing through Paris, with a CND Petition to deliver to The Big Three concerning World Disarmament, on my way to May-June in Basel. Robin Sharp (and later Brian Duckworth) met with me, and we decided to form the Methodist Renewal Group. From 1961 to 1970, this was a collegial seed-bed for progressive thinking and practice. The first Conferences at Birmingham in January and at Greyladies, Southwark in May brought 14 of us together. Nine annual conferences ended with 60 present. The first members were Geoffrey Ainger, Raymond Billington, Kenneth Cracknell, Norwyn Denny, Pauline Webb, Brian Duckworth, David Head, Donald Henry, Richard Jones, John Kent, David Mason, Tom Patton, Henry Rack, Robin Sharp, Peter Stephens, Alan Tongue, Peter Watkin and myself. Twenty eight then joined in January 1962, giving a membership by 1970 of 80.

The ethos of the Renewal Group was celebrated in *Beware The Church*, edited by John M. Waterhouse,(1968) in which we published essays on Mission and Evangelism (Brian Duckworth), Worship (Trevor Rowe), Learning to Care (Norwyn Denny), "Stop The World I Want To Get Off" (Brian Frost) and "Good Seed, Stony Ground" (by myself). I reflected that "Methodism had so far not proved itself outstandingly good ground for the good seed" – though "Those outside seem to fare no better" (p.19)

ASHRAM COMMUNITY

The formation of Ashram Community in 1967 owed a great deal to Iona. As a student and then a young minister, I had been to Iona from 1958 several times and, in 1963 led a week on "Renewal in Methodism" and in 1970 a week on "Community Today" with other Ashram members. I led Community Weeks in Iona Abbey, and all our family lived at Dunsmeorach, our friend, George MacLeod's home, while he lived in the Abbey Vestry to make that possible.

When I told Donald Soper in the early 1960s that I felt called to found some kind of Urban Christian Community, he said, "I can't help you there. Go to George MacLeod". Long talks with George led to clarification and alternative vocations. Ashram wanted to be based in inner cities, not on an island, wanted to be *Honest to God* Theology rather than in Celtic Mysticism. George accepted all this and helped, on many occasions with Ashram Community and later Urban Theology Unit. In July 1969, I became a Co-sponsor in George's (failed!) *"New Breakthrough in Christ"*. In March 1972 he dedicated Emmaus House, UTU's temporary base, and in August I led a week on "Radical Methodism" on Iona.

Ashram held its inaugural meeting in July 1967, in the Champness Hall, Rochdale. In January 1970 we opened our first Community House in Rochdale, and others followed in Sheffield, Middlesbrough, Birmingham and London, and later in Glasgow and Stockton. Since 1967 we have had between 70 and 120 Members and Associates. In 2017 we have 40 Members and 40 Associates, with 5 regional Branches and in Sheffield 5 Community Houses and 2 Shop centres with accommodation. In Burngreave we have accommodation for 6, asylum seekers included. Ashram's basic elements set down in the early 1970s have remained with us in various forms, as recent publications indicate.

Ashram's most public product was *Journey: Explorations into Discipleship*, published in 2001 as a radical and Jesus-centred alternative to the widespread Alpha Course. *Journey* and its supplementary booklets sold 4,000 copies, and still is used for group and personal study by those wanting to find a faith which is both practical and contemporary, and based on Jesus of the Gospels.

A history up to 2009 is in *A Lifestyle of Sharing*. Its bi-annual *ACT Together* and its Annual Reports continue the story up to today. Its 50th Anniversary in 2017 brought us back to Champness Hall for a Reunion Day, on May 6th .

ALLIANCE OF RADICAL METHODISTS

At its Whitsun Conference of 1970, the Renewal Group decided to merge with other denominational groups to form "One for Christian Renewal." In a long walk along the seashore at Scarborough, where we were meeting, Norwyn Denny and I decided that we would seek others to join in a continuing Methodist Group to be called the Alliance of Radical Methodists. We called a first conference, and soon David Haslam, Clive Scott, Brian Jenner, Roger Hutchings, Geoff Reid, Ronald Gibbins, Roy Crowder, David Moore and others joined us. The life of ARM, especially its annual

38

appearances at the Methodist Conference, and its *Armprint* Daily Newssheet there, brought life and controversy to Conference for the next decades, 1971 to 2000.

ARM pioneered and got through Conference some radical and progressive proposals, and was always a lively and open community of debate. However, it seemed to become a platform for anyone with a "radical" idea, and fell victim of endless internal debates. It certainly was the case that in the end COSPEC produced more useful results in many instances. There is a negative side to radicalism, which is endlessly pouncing on others because of things done or not done. That kind of radicalism has never been of interest to me.

CHRISTIAN ORGANISATIONS FOR SOCIAL, POLITICAL AND ECONOMIC CHANGE

In 1980 I called a meeting of the leaders of some of the politically inclined groups - SCM. Iona, Christian CND, Christian Action, Pax Christi, Alliance of Radical Methodists, Christian Socialist Movement, Urban Theology Unit and Ashram Community. John Atherton came, but feared we were Socialist. Edward Charles from Jubilee Group was a supporter. Simon Barrow became Co-ordinator. Grace was Treasurer.

COSPEC met several times each year, and discussed what we together as Christian groups could do politically. In Autumn 1980, we had a special issue of *Christian Action*, in 1982, SCM published *COSPEC Stories*, in 1984, UTU published our *Insights for Christian Opposition*, and in 1985 an *Alternative Election Manifesto*. This represented significant output for a small voluntary group. But we had not sufficient resources or people, and closed in 1989.

COSPEC demonstrated two things at least. First, the fragility of all Christian movements. We rightly deem that "Small is Beautiful". But the tragedy of the 30 or so organisations which constituted COSPEC was that they simply could not afford either money or volunteers (none had long-term paid staff) to make serious consistent campaigning possible.

The second thing demonstrated was that Socialism was in dispute. At the Inaugural Meeting, John Atherton, (before recent moves into radically different directions!) argued that we ought to have "Socialist" in our title. But we decided against it, in favour of "Social, Political and Economic Change". Was New Labour in 2000 a further withdrawal from Socialism? And Christian Socialist Movement's change to being "Christians of the Left" in 2010?

On my six "Start – Ups", I commented in *A Lifestyle of Sharing*: "Looking back, it would clearly have been better and more noticeable and significant if all these very messy, bitty and relatively fragile pieces of endeavour had been put under one prominent banner. We might have been noticed more, and the drain of organisation, maintenance and membership gathering would certainly have been less. Yet it was the time of "Small is Beautiful", and each of the groupings and associations served rather special needs, projects and people. I became, the "chief cook and bottle washer" for all four, and encouraged them all to grow along separate if related paths. At least you could join what took your fancy rather than have to swallow a conglomerate 'John Vincent's Show'" (p.19).

Reference.

John Vincent, Journey: *Explorations into Discipleship*. Rev.Ed. 2003; Journey: *Resource Book*. 2003 (2 Volumes together £6) Sheffield Ashram Press

8

INNER CITY

John

The Rochdale Methodist Mission based in the Champness Hall was Joseph Rank's 1927 response to an Appeal for a Mission Hall by Rochdale Cotton Mill owners, the Samuel Heaps. George Heap was Circuit Steward before and during my years there. On one occasion, George declared to me "To start anything, the first thing you have to do is to bottom it.". "Bottoming it" became for me a contemporary aspect of Incarnation – and "start-ups" my response. But then, somewhere, Digging in Deep. But where?

I returned from New York in May 1970, with outline plans to set up the Urban Theology Unit in England. While still trying to firm up these plans, largely with David Mason in London, the Methodist Conference met in July in the Whitworth Hall of Manchester University. There, a special committee was formed to look at my plans, and several long term allies went to it in support- David Mason, Pauline Webb, Brian Duckworth, Ron Marshall, Harry Morton.

But the Conference in an hour long debate on the Friday, including a critical speech, clever but unsupportive, from Donald Soper, voted not to give me "Permission to Serve" with the UTU – which admittedly was mainly schemes rather than reality. UTU had in fact only been formed by myself and three friends – Tony Wesson, David Mason and Roland Seaman – in September 1969, just before I left for Boston. "You just ruined this man's ministry" shouted Ron Marshall to Donald Soper on the way out. But in Methodism, by the end of Conference, every minister must be "stationed". A small group of senior friends of mine met to find me a place. After an hour's deliberation, Walker Lee, Kenneth Waights, Percy Scott and Frank

Amery came out and told me what they had decided - four inner city churches in the Sheffield North Circuit. Eric Baker, Donald Soper and Irvonwy Morgan were already discussing a London base for me for 1971. But in reality I knew that once I got into anywhere, I would get committed to it. Any Inner City "Bottom" would do.

SHEFFIELD

The family was unimpressed. They knew I had been offered university professorships (In USA and Hawaii) and other central mission superintendencies. Faith said, "You didn't have to bring us to this dump, Dad."

In Sheffield we were in the midst of a situation of decline, disillusionment and departure by the upwardly mobile. However, five days after our arrival in the manse at 239 Abbeyfield Road, Mike Newton brought two young City Councillors round to see me – David Blunkett and Francis Butler, both Methodist Local Preachers On Trial, one Labour and one Liberal. Their plea was unanimous. "We know you didn't want to come here", they said. "But there is vital work for you to do here. We want you to stay. And we will work with you."

All three kept their word. Indeed, the four of us very soon formed the Pitsmoor Action Group, to start dealing with pressing local issues, including plans to demolish our whole area, which an Andover Street Ashram House campaign finally got reversed in 1972.

URBAN THEOLOGY UNIT

First, we slowly got UTU going in our spare time, until we could buy our first house in December 1973, Pitsmoor Study House, at 210 Abbeyfield Road. We got the £7,000 needed from friends (£1,000), the City Council (£3,000 – to do local community work) and the Society of the Sacred Mission (£3,000 as a loan, later turned into a gift). The only models I had were the then Alternative Theological Seminary in Washington DC, the Dissenting Academics of 17th Century England, and Dietrich Bonhoeffer's Finkenwalde Seminary of 1935-37, plus John Wesley's model at the New Room in Bristol – teaching room, plus library and accommodation.

Second, we got Ashram going, in September 1971, opening our first Sheffield Community House at 84 Andover Street, with a brilliant team of people in their twenties – Roy Crowder, Howard Knight, Raymond Hinch and Rita Norris were the first members.

42

Much of the ideas and histories of UTU and Ashram are in recent books – *Christ in the City* for UTU, and *A Lifestyle of Sharing* for Ashram Community.

SHEFFIELD INNER CITY ECUMENICAL MISSION

The third innovation was the Sheffield Inner City Ecumenical Mission, started in September 1971. This created an umbrella for small struggling churches and projects, including UTU and Ashram. In 10 years, we had developed into a broad-based mutual fellowship, with ten different churches, denominations, memberships and buildings, each with their attendant projects.

Ian Lucraft, our pioneering colleague from 1973, described our policy as "supporting the traditional, and expecting the experimental". We had an ecumenical sponsoring committee, which the very supportive Frank Amery, the District Chair convened, and a ten year fruitful colleagueship with a URC minister, Duncan Wilson.

We made churches viable and credible by securing alternative premises – Pitsmoor moved into a housing complex, Grimesthorpe into a corner shop, Lopham Street into a local public house, the Furnival. Richard Caborn MP and his mother came to the latter's opening in 1995, and a brilliant Baptist Minister Jane Grinonneau, in September moved into a council flat on the block to start into a seven year ministry.

In all this, I am attempting to be at the same time a student and disciple of Jesus and of Jesus stories as contained in the Gospels, and also a Community Worker on the streets of the Inner City. Indeed, I argue in *Radical Jesus* that the street level community worker today is what the Jesus of first century Palestine translates into in contemporary Britain.

GOSPEL "TESTAMENTS"

I found myself as a Theologian, interpreting and expecting aspects of the Way and work of Jesus and his Disciples described in the Gospels to be actually working out in our inner city mission activities and attitudes. *Into the City,* (1982) has a "Gospel Pattern" thus:

43

Gospel Mark	Practical Implications	SICEM Example
Incarnation	Living in the Midst	Inner City Sheffield
Healings	Doing things in locality	Sheffield Inner City Ecumenical Mission
Parables	Putting up visible signs	Ashram House, Pitsmoor Meth.Ch. Urban Theology Unit
Acted Parables	Developing alternatives	Town Planning, Community Projects
Disciple Groups	Small, poor, indigenous	Eucharist Congregation, St. James URC, Wincobank Chapel
Crucifixion	Oppression by outsiders	Grimesthorpe Shop Church
Resurrection	Alternative Journeys	Downwards, Backwards, Sideways
New Jerusalem	Radical Politics in Society	Neighbourhood Government

In a second book on inner city mission, *Hope from the City*, published in 2000, I develop the Gospel Models idea in terms of specific Gospel stories. Thus, the various chapters tell of our study of a Gospel passage, and then a story or stories about how they seem to get a *reprise* in the life of a particular Church, community, practice or incident. In each case, a familiar inner city "problem" is the starting-point: and a story from a SICEM branch is an illustration or experimental embodiment – our present day "Testament"

To support all this, we worked at "Spiritualities and Strategies for Christians and Churches": SICEM Half Days, the model of "Twos and Threes", a Team Ministry, Disciplines for Missioners, and a Seminary of the Streets (UTU).

SEMINARY OF THE STREETS

Urban Theology Unit as the "Seminary of the Streets" was the supportive "Think Tank" and the experimental Training Ground for all

44

this. From 1971 to 1999, we had ten to twenty people of all ages, backgrounds and countries on the UTU 9 - month "Study Year", which helped create intentional ministries by many people, both around Britain and around the world. Part-time Urban Ministry courses, plus 137 Masters and Doctors degrees, for which I was Supervisor or Joint Supervisor, developed the method, which owed much to the teaching of the New York Theological Seminary DMin (1978-1990).

Our UTU MPhil/PhD is in Contextual, Urban and Liberation Theologies, and its development has gained from work with colleagues in the two University Departments in which I was an Honorary Lecturer and Doctoral Supervisor – Sheffield University Department of Biblical Studies (1991-2016) and Birmingham University Department of Theology and Religion (2004-2018). These UTU programmes now continue through Luther King House of Manchester University, also an MA in Contextual Theology.

I have continued with UTU as lecturer and supervisior for MPhil/PhDs with Ian Duffield, and with the July summer schools, and other tasks including publications. In 1991-2000, I worked for periods in Australia, at Parramata Urban Institute, Wooloomooloo Inner City Mission, and at the Sydney United Theological Seminary. From 1990-2015, I worked with Don Rudalevige in USA and Sheffield on their Urban Mission Training Project.

Since ceasing to be full-time employed in SICEM and UTU in 1997, I have worked with other community committed practitioners, and seen how these methods work for them. The first result of this, after periods with urban ministers at St. Deiniol's Library, Hawarden, was published as *Faithfulness in the City* (2003). The second result was been the publication of a book I edited on Personal and Community Responses to Gospel passages, in *Mark: Gospel in Action* (SPCK 2006). This now continues with annual volumes of "*Gospel Practice Interpretation*", published since 2011 by Deo Publishing, often resulting from the UTU/Ashram Summer School.

Each academic year since 1991, I have sent in to Sheffield University and Birmingham University a report on lectures given. Subjects in 2006-2007 indicate the concerns and the issues: "Practice Criticism of Mark's Gospel". British New Testament Conference, Sheffield, 4 September. "Christianity and Politics", Donald Soper Lecture, Hinde Street Methodist Church, 28 January; "Living with Mark's Gospel". Student Christian Movement Conference, Cleobury

45

Mortimer 16-18 February; "Faithful Cities in Perspective". Urban Studies Department, Nazarene College, Manchester, 6 March; "Regeneration: An Alternative Renaissance", Lord Mayor's Seminar, Town Hall, Sheffield, 16 March; "Practice Criticism", Bible and Society Group, Mansfield College, Oxford, 29-30 March; "Practice Interpretation", Scripture Studies seminar, Newman College, Birmingham, 22 May.

THEOLOGIAN AND MISSIONER

In these ways, I endeavour to continue the dual roles of New Testament Interpreter, and of Practical Urban Missioner, to which I first committed myself on returning from Basel in 1956.

In 2017, the first role is continued in my work with doctoral and ministerial students and with organising conferences and working parties, especially on Practice Interpretation. The Urban Theology Unit is now located in Victoria Hall in Sheffield, where I go usually for one or two mornings each week. The second role is continued through the Sheffield Houses and Projects of Ashram Community, especially at the multi-project Burngreave Ashram at 80-86 Spital Hill, where our Community Projects base hosts accommodation for asylum seekers and students, a Multi-Faith Chapel and Library, a weekly Free Meal for those in need, with food from supermarkets through FareShare, plus whatever other community activities we can get groups to come and organise.

In my experience, these two roles are both required in the world today. My conviction remains that if you dig deep into Christianity and the Gospels you come out with vocation, lifestyle change and mission with the poor. Equally if you dig deep into social, economic and political questions you come out with the road to radical alternatives, such as Christianity and the Gospels provide

In 2018, Keith Hebden the new Director of Urban Theology Unit starts a yearly 5 - week summer Community Theologian Internship Programme. Burngreave Ashram is arranging one of the first "takers". Also, now nationally we are called Urban Theology Union.

9

STEEL CITY VILLAGE

Grace

Grimesthorpe is a typical working class, 19th century community, walking distance from the steel works, a steel city village.

Wesley Hall, Grimesthorpe, joined SICEM in 1972, and I moved my membership there from Pitsmoor. With June Clark, I ran a Friday evening Sunday School. In 1978, we managed to sell the big old building and bought two shops. 41-43 Birdwell Road.

There was a single room in the corner shop, large enough for table tennis or square tables to seat 20 at the lunch club. Off this led a smaller "front room", the Chapel, which had our communion furniture, a piano, and sixteen chairs around the walls. Behind this room, leading off the larger room is the kitchen. Upstairs was a flat to house 2 or 3 volunteer residents.

SHOP CHURCH

We opened the "Shop Centre" on 15 June 1980. The first Residents were Margaret Mackley, Richard Levitt and Mark Woodhead. The original "Statement of Aims" stated that the purpose of the Shop Centre was:

1. To provide self-contained accommodation for two to three mission workers

2. To provide small premises for weekday and Sunday church activities and services

3. To provide a shop, store, community facility, craft centre and/or coffee bar, to give the mission a shop window and a meeting point with local people.

Our idea was to create a street level place to meet, where various services to the community could exist side by side with an explicitly Christian community, doing its own thing and creating a new generation of disciples. (*Into the City,* p.101)

Since 1980, over the years, around twenty people in their twenties have come and lived in the flat and worked with us, usually joining the congregation.

The Sunday service was thoroughly participatory, with no-one being too shy to join in. We happily sang unaccompanied but several people could play the piano. Bible readings were read around the room. Intercessions were talked about, and the sermon was often a "congregational sermon", with everyone joining in who wished. Children were welcome to come in and show us what they were doing.

CHARACTERISTICS OF CHURCH

It seems to me that there are three significant and essential characteristics of this kind of church.

First, the room and the numbers are both small. In what larger churches would old or shy and inarticulate people feel free to contribute? Because we know each other well, there is no artificial, formal talk. Conversation is real and about real things, and rarely in "religious" language. Secondly, there is a basic assumption that we are all in this together, that everyone is valued and takes responsibility for what happens. So their thoughts are heard. It is a corporate ministry of all members. Thirdly, the understanding is that we are there for each other, for the children, for the local community, and for the whole world. The context is tiny but the brief is vast.

We almost invariably went home stronger and affirmed in our faith, not because we had heard a good sermon (which we certainly often did), but because the disciples of Jesus had been building each other up for our work in the world.

John says that his teacher, Karl Barth, said that a Church is a provisional demonstration of what is intended for all humanity. At times, we were!

Unfortunately, changes in SICEM policy, and our failure to continue to find adequate flat residents or chapel workers led to closure. We celebrated with a Thanksgiving in July 2006.

10

PEOPLE'S BANK

John

In December 1984 Grace and I chanced to see a Diverse Reports programme on Channel 4 by Christopher Hird which first alerted us to the fact that large and fundamental changes were being planned for the Trustee Savings Bank, with whom we ourselves and all our organisations banked as a matter of principle, as it belonged to its depositors. Christopher Hird sent us the script of his programme. On 16th January 1985, we wrote to our local TSB Manager on Spital Hill voicing our concerns at the proposed privatisation and asking him to come and meet some of us to talk about it. We received a copy of the Government White Paper and a calming letter advising us that most speculation on such major changes was ill-informed and that it was all "only proposals". We wrote to the *Guardian* on 9th February 1985, the letter starting a national process.

Very reluctantly, we began to realise that the mantle had fallen on us. No-one else had emerged. We were going to have to get in there and fight. For ten days we prevaricated. We had no time, we were already too heavily committed on numerous fronts, but we knew we had to do it. We could do no other.

So in October 1985, we lifted the phone to a solicitor in our own inner city area who was a "radical". The result was decisive. John Howell was highly interested in the tentative question about taking on the TSB. We pointed out that we had no money. He said, "It won't be the first time I worked for no money.

HIGH COURT WRIT

With John, we formulated a simple plan in which eight TSB members would take the TSB to court, alleging that the proposed privatisation took away assets which were properly theirs as Depositors. Already in 1973, a Government Committee chaired by Sir Harry Page had recommended not capitalisation but rather Mutual Bank status. To our amazement, on 18th December 1985 John Howell received a High Court writ addressed to Rev. John J. Vincent seeking:-

1. A Declaration that the depositors of Trustee Savings Bank England and Wales are entitled, in accordance with the terms applicable to their respective accounts with the Bank, to repayment of the principal amounts credited to such accounts and, in the case of interest thereon at the rates from time to time applicable thereto, but have no present or future, actual or contingent right, title or interest to the assets of the Bank.

2. An order that John J. Vincent, the First Defendant herein, be appointed to represent all other depositors of Trustee Savings Bank England and Wales.

3. Further or other relief

4. That provision may be made for the costs of this application.

Without a doubt, the TSB knew that in moving to sell on the Stock Market a bank whose ownership was unknown, they were on very shallow ground indeed. They had declared categorically: "The TSBs do not belong to the Government, nor do they belong to the Trustees, to their employees, or to the depositors". (TSB Annual Report 1986).

TSB DEPOSITORS ASSOCIATION

None of this had been proven in the Courts. Now one of these possible groups of owners were contending for rights of ownership. In Scotland, their right had been debated. They could have a good case, which would jeopardise TSB's enormous investment already made towards flotation. Here, the TSB decided to pay all costs to prove their point in the High Court. In turn, in February 1986, with Grace as Secretary and myself as Chair, we formed a TSB Depositors Association. We described our purpose thus- "The Association is being formed in order to provide a means of communication and mutual support for all members of the Trustee Savings Bank who wish to secure the future of the TSB as we have known it, and as we believe it would develop"

We outlined actions so far and our prime argument, and urged depositors to find new members and gain us publicity through the media by letters and articles. We asked a minimum of £2 subscription, but without publicity we only gained 80 members. Yet we continued to get a stream of letters from TSB staff and depositors. An appearance on "Newsnight" helped.

HIGH COURT HEARING

So Grace and I went to London with John Howell, at the TSB's expense. At the outset of the High Court case, on 28 April 1986, I made a statement, parts of which were as follows:

"The Depositors of the TSB do not desire to claim for themselves any part of the Bank's present or future assets. This is because we believe that no-one has any "right, title or interest" that they might "cash in" on what the Bank has become. Our concerns are much deeper. "First, it seems to me that the Trustee Savings Bank is precisely and simply what the name implies. It is a bank for the savings of people for which other persons undertake to be Trustees, guaranteeing to return their invested money plus interest, when requested. The Trustees at no stage become the owners of the money of others given into their trust.

"This simple layman's understanding of Trusteeship is one with which, as a Methodist minister, I am very familiar. I am also aware that under Charity law, no Trustee is allowed to use either the capital or the interest of monies entrusted to him for personal gain. It seems to me that this fundamental nature of disinterested Trusteeship must now be categorically affirmed. I believe that this is a vital step, to serve the many parts of our national life held in Trusteeship.

"Secondly, it seems to me that it is not permitted to Trustees basically to change the nature of what is put in their trust. We believe further that if they are in danger of doing this, they should be legally prevented.

"Thirdly, I am concerned that the original purpose of the Trustee Savings Bank will be lost. This original purpose was to provide a savings bank for the poor. This is abundantly clear from all the formal documents from 1819 onwards.

"Today, Britain is becoming more and more a divided country. I want to ensure that the Trustee Savings Bank will continue to be present in our inner city areas, council housing estates, small villages and less prosperous areas of the country. Once the Bank has to show dividends on the Stock Exchange, comparable to those of other High Street Banks, these social and philanthropic prerequisites of the Bank cannot be assured."

I concluded: "I am also concerned that an Institution which has been content to remain in a certain degree of uncertainty about its nature is now being forced to fit in with other standard institutions. This is a wider problem for all society. But I believe the Court should act in the light of it."

Grace and myself, with John Howell, stayed at the Russell Square Hotel, and had lunches with Joshua Rozenburg, the BBC Legal Correspondent, who followed it all with great interest.

All my points were debated by Judge Scott in his Statement. Indeed, in his Summing up Declaration, he declared (1) "Depositors are entitled to repayments and interest", but more significantly, (2) "The assets of the said Bank are held subject to the statutory provisions and rules for the time being in force upon trust to provide for payment to depositors of the sums due to them."

In other words, Judge Scott was saying that the "assets" could only be used to pay depositors their dues – nothing more, and nothing else. At the end, I asked Sir John Reid, Chairman of TSB, where he thought this left us. "Sixty –forty", he replied, "sixty to us but forty to you".

EARLY DAY MOTION

Plainly the matter was not settled. We had long discussions with MP, Richard Caborn. And I persuaded an old Methodist friend, John Hicks QC, to take our case. To get the case more widely understood, Grace and I published a large four page document, *TSB: the New Future*, part of which was widely quoted. Richard Caborn got five other MPs, to put in a House of Commons Early Day Motion as follows:

"Future of the TSB". That this House welcomes the publication of the Report *TSB: the New Future*, by Dr. John and Mrs Grace

Vincent, published by the TSB Depositors Association of England and Wales; and believes the alternative future proposed by the Report is faithful to TSB's history and will make a significant contribution to the life of the nation. "The EDM got over 130 signatures.

HOUSE OF LORDS

So we had to go to the House of Lords to sort it out. On June 17, John Howell sent me a document. The situation was stated as: "Dr Vincent brings his appeal in respect of the first declaration (1). The Central Board and the Custodian Trustees of TSB cross appeal in respect of the second declaration (2)."

The key question was whether assets of the bank as a whole could be separated from the depositors' investments held in Trust. Until this was clear, "HM Treasury has declined to appoint the vesting day while the issues raised in these proceedings remain to be finally determined by Your Lordship's House."

The appeal from the TSB was that their Lordships should set aside Judge Scott's second point about assets, for various reasons especially "(5) because the Learned Judge was in error in finding that there was a fiduciary relationship between the depositors and the Bank and its depositors however limited in nature", and "(6) because the relationship between the Bank and its depositors is contractual. The depositors have contractual rights and have no interest in the asset of the Bank."

Five days of debate before five Law Lords followed. One, Lord Templeton, finally produced the nonsense which could have helped our case, unintentionally: "In 1819 the Savings Bank was effectively nationalised." But the findings stuck to old simplicities we had never questioned, that depositors do not own assets, without asking our constant question that no-one else does, least of all Trustees.

BANKING FOR PEOPLE

All this got us frequently on radio, TV, and in the national press. A sobering experience!

Much to the local TSB's surprise (their branch was on the corner opposite to Burngreave Ashram!), we and all our SICEM Branches stayed with TSB. And we are still there. Though it is a peculiar irony that in 2014 the investment part of Lloyds/TSB, as it by then had become, was hived off and called TSB, while our local branches have become the total opposite of the neighbourhood people's bank, and are now called Lloyds!

When I was at school at MGS, I used occasionally to walk from Oxford Road station to Rusholme, and spend the money saved on *The Manchester Guardian*. Now, we find even the Saturday weekly *Guardian* read more than enough!

But then, in the midst of so much "keeping up with the *Sun*" journalism, you get occasional pieces faithful to the tradition. So on 23 August 2014 I find James Meek writing on "Sale of the Century". TSB is just one of a long list of "privatised industries and public sector services". "The notion that greed on the part of a private executive elite is the chief and sufficient engine of prosperity for all" rules out everything else – including TSB.

In the end, the TSB experience made one conclude that there was no way that historical or moral arguments could or would triumph over immediate commercial or banking interests. But I would have one more bash at it – as the Methodist President.

The question remains for us in 2017, in even sharper form. Can there ever be – as TSB claimed – a People's Bank?

11

SHOP FOR JUSTICE

Grace

In 1982 it so happened that residents had moved on from the Ashram House in Andover Street Burngreave, and there was only one left. This was normal and not a problem as we could have found more.

But it set us thinking. What about opening a house somewhere on the West side of the city where we could attract a different style of member and where we could raise some of the issues confronting us in the inner city? Ideally it would be somewhere visible, perhaps on a busy street.

And in 1987 we found it! Not just a house but a shop on Glossop Road, Sheffield, just between the University and the Hallamshire Hospital. It was a fruit and vegetable shop and the seller was very kind in helping us to take it over, as none of us had any experience in running a business. There were about 10 of us. He taught us how to use the till and took me to learn to buy at the 6am fruit and vegetable wholesale market!

Then we quickly expanded what he had sold into a range of wholefoods, pasties and Traidcraft. Our policy was to be all vegetarian, as much vegan as possible and as local and ethical as possible. And we would use the big front window for all sorts of displays on a wide range of issues and social concerns, allowing other groups to use it too.

VOLUNTEERS

We have never had difficulty finding volunteers to run the shop, particularly students. And we need 15-20 a week!

There is an excellent flat upstairs which has always been very easy to fill and we have had a wonderful range of people there over the years, all involved in the work, from the first residents in 1987.

The whole project worked to fulfil a scheme proposed earlier which described its purpose thus: "The project aims to provide a Christian Community Centre in an inner city area of Sheffield's west end (Broomhall) and a 'shop window' for the activities of Ashram Community; a meeting place for organisations involved in social, and political actions; and a practical workshop, publicity outlet and a 'launching pad' for community initiatives."

It is a 'Shop for Justice' not a shop for profit. From 1987 to 2013, I was the one to hold it all together. In 2013 I was not well, and we needed new leadership. In some desperation and not much hope we advertised for volunteers to take it on. Amazingly, in September 2013 two dynamic young men, Joe Thompson and Joe Davies, moved in and radically developed the project, in terms of the building, new volunteers and a new vision. All this transformed everything, bringing in more customers and creating more interest in what we are about, and bringing in many more student volunteers. Since August 2014, Dave Judge, and Dave Westley took over, in September 2015 Dan Robinson and Rosie Benson followed, and in September 2016. Jake Gresham and Joe Russell. All have been brilliant.

GOOD NEWS FROM A SHOP

A booklet I wrote called *New Roots; Shop for Justice* concluded with a chapter, "Good News from a Shop". The following section headings give a good idea of the thinking and purpose behind all we do there.

1.Returning to the Street
2.Raising the Significance of Everyday Things
3.Acting Justly
4.Standing for Something
5.Believing in the Power of Quite Simple Choices
6.Declaring our Interdependence as Human Beings
7.Deliberately Creating Oddity and Provocative Juxtaposition
8.Exposing the Hidden Connections
9.Acknowledging the Complexities

10.Asserting that all Things Hold Together

We kept all this in a 3rd Edition, published in 2015

AT SPITAL HILL

In 2000, John and I began to think about developing a similar project to New Roots in Burngreave. So we looked around Spital Hill.

We went in to see Keith Laycock, whom we knew, in his jewellery and watch shop. "What do you think Keith?" "Come and look" he said. He showed us a whole range of buildings, including a possible shop next door. He had bought them as security for his shop and they were not for sale. "But you can have them", he said, "I know you. I think they cost me £82k and you can have them for that." Amazing! Of course we said "yes"! We had just sold the Ashram Community House in Sparkbrook, Birmingham; which helped put up the £82K.

So from 2004-2012 we ran a simple version of New Roots, as a Cafe. Sadly we had to close that in the summer of 2012 as the trade was so poor.

BURNGREAVE BANQUET – FREE MEAL

But we then developed it as a Community Space, where different groups meet and where we do our Burngreave Banquet or Free Meal on a Wednesday evening.

This Free Meal on Wednesday serves 25-30 hungry people. It is cooked by local Ashram friends with food received from FareShare, an organisation which collects unwanted food from supermarkets. It has become a real community meeting event.

After the free Banquet; half a dozen of the volunteers plus a few guests go down to our Multi-Faith Chapel and share a Eucharist, led by each of us in turn. And we reflect. Is this the Lord' s Supper we have down here in the cellar Chapel? And was it not also the Lord's Supper that we all shared in the upstairs Cafe? Both are, of course!

Then in 2015, Ros Norsworthy completed her brilliant large painting. She titles it: "Christ in Burngreave: the Lord's Supper at the Burngreave Ashram Free Meal".

NAMIBIA HOUSE

Another project that involved myself as organizer / secretary was Namibia House. In 1981, we had a mature student Magdalena Hoebes, doing the UTU Study Year, and through this we became involved in the plight of her children, and then of others, who came as refugees from Namibia. So we adapted 233 Abbeyfield Road, which we owned, for use by Namibian refugees, and in the end were providing home and safety to up to six residents at a time. John Mellor, a retired Methodist headmaster from Zimbabwe, plus Jackie, Francis Butler's wife, joined us in a small Trustees Group, which devoted itself to the house. In January 1991, John was invited to Windhoek for the Independence Celebrations of the new Namibia and met several of our former house members. John in turn was feited by local Methodists, whose Bishop took him to chat with Nelson Mandela. By then Namibia House had done its job, closing in 1992.

12

NATIONAL VOICE

John

"KING METH"

From 1963, I had become regularly an elected member of the annual Methodist Conference, in fact for five periods as a "Conference elected" member which then lasts for three year stints. In 1965, I presented a major and very controversial reinterpretation of Methodism in my book, *Christ and Methodism*. In 1966, I persuaded Conference to appoint a Commission on the Church's Ministries in the Modern World, which reported in 1968, with further reports in 1971. My *Fellowship of the Kingdom* Study Booklet, *Ministry Today and Tomorrow* (1974) summarises the work.

Pauline Webb was Vice-President in 1965, and Harry Morton (1972) and Colin Morris (1976) Presidents. But they were hard years for radicals. After several key resignations or exclusions, in 1968, Colin Morris grabbed me and asked, "Who's up for crucifixion this year, John?". The 1970's saw me fighting for our new perspectives based on our "Digging In". In 1973, the then President, Donald Lee, got me to address Conference on "What is Happening". I delivered "Strategies for Mission" lectures in Adelaide in August 1976 in the midst of six weeks lecturing across the USA, New Zealand, Australia and Singapore. Every summer I lectured in USA, partly to get money for UTU to pay its "assessment". The five four-week spells teaching on the Drew University D.Min (1979 – 1983) also opened up their MDiv students to the chance to do The Study Year at UTU, which eight did over 5 years.

Personally, I had moved from being dubbed (in the *Methodist Recorder* and elsewhere) Methodism's "*enfant terrible*" in the 1950's to its "Maverick" in the 1960's, to being "Methodism's Tony Benn" (Edwards Rogers' phrase) in the 1970's. But what would Methodism do with such a figure?

In 1980, the Conference met in Sheffield, and I got a Working Group appointed on "Two Nations – One Gospel?" which published a report in 1981. We also got an Inner City Committee together, and in 1983 launched the Methodist Mission Alongside the Poor. "Alongside" was my word.

Meantime, I continued with Radio and TV, as time permitted, and published books. *OK Let's be Methodists* in 1984 caused a little stir, with its plea to return – or advance – to the radicalism of Wesley.

All this meant that by 1988 my name had appeared in the Nominations for President of Conference, and I was duly elected in London in July 1988, and took office at the Conference at De Montfort Hall in Leicester on 24th June 1989. All the family was there, and our son-in-law Tony coined the title "King Meth".

PRESIDENTIAL ADDRESS

My Presidential Address took its key from the national mood of the time. The social and economic suffering that had resulted from Mrs Thatcher's policies emerged. In the Conference of 1988, we agreed eight Resolutions of Protest. The President, Dr Richard G. Jones, was instructed to seek an interview with the Prime Minister. I wrote to the *Methodist Recorder* on 21st July 1988 of a Methodism "United in Outrage at what is Happening to our Nation."

Methodist minister Gordon Webster's cartoon indicates how Mrs Thatcher reacted – not knowing that I was in the waiting! (*Methodist Recorder*, June 1989) (see below p.96).

I called my Presidential Address in June 1989, "The Five Pillars of Christianity". I outlined these as

- A Worldly God
- A New Reality
- Priority for the Poor
- Journey Downwards
- Things in Common

Most of the address concerned the scriptural and theological justifications for these, and what they meant for individual disciples and for the Church. But I also applied them to politics, particularly taking up the claims of Mrs Thatcher and others that their philosophy and policies were Christian.

The Worldly God, I said, meant that Christianity's prime concern was with the life of the world, with people deciding their own destinies, not being kept passive.

The New Reality of the Kingdom of God now present on earth meant, indeed, that (as Mrs Thatcther had said at the Scottish Church Assembly) "Abundance rather than poverty has legitimacy which derives from the very nature of creation". But that meant Abundance for all, not just for some.

The Priority for the Poor meant that the way the poor are treated is the test of the greatness of a nation. The "trickle down" theory had simply not worked, while the Poll Tax simply victimised the poor.

I concluded that politics and politicians and the wealthy needed to take a "Journey Downwards", to free up investment and services for the development of all; and that rather than saying that "there is no such thing as society, but only individuals and families", as Mrs Thatcher did, we should be working towards a Society in which as much as possible would be "In Common".

Conference repeated the appeal to Mrs Thatcher to meet myself and the ex-President. In the end, she said "No!" So on 6 December 1989, Dick Jones, Brian Beck, Brian Duckworth and I delivered "An Open Letter to the Prime Minister" at 10 Downing Street. For more on this, see *Discipleship in the 90s* (1991), pp 34-43.

PRESIDENTIAL YEAR

The Methodist Presidency gives one a chance in a lifetime to take centre stage in the denomination, and get noticed and quoted in the media. Brian Frost comments that "Every President brings to the post a particular style", and goes on "A number, W.E. Sangster, Colin Morris, John Vincent, were really themselves 'writ large'."

It has been the custom of Presidents to spend 4 days in visits to the Districts, covering half each year. Having very heavy responsibilities still in SICEM and UTU, I planned shorter visits, wherever possible catching a late night Sunday train back, so that I was back at my desk on a Monday morning. My major events, conducted in almost all Districts, were Saturday Conferences on "Britain in the Nineties", to which everyone was invited, including local MPs and Civic officers, as well as Church leaders and bishops – some of whom came. All this public ministry was made possible by the brilliant Brian Beck, who as Secretary of Conference kept the Church on an even keel, and attended the rather numerous events (especially Anglican ones!) for which I as President could not really justify another trip (especially to London!).

The Day Conferences from 10 am to around 3 or 4 pm, were often heated! I repeated some of my Presidential Address points, which provoked some bitter response. I especially recall a Saturday in London South West District, when local Conservatives turned out in force. Even worse was a Birmingham District Saturday event, at Solihull, which became so heated that at 3 pm the District Chair, Donald Eadie, declared "Come on John, I am getting you out of this. They are just not listening".

If anyone wanted to follow up on what I was saying, they were invited to six Mission and Vocation weekends in Sheffield, and also a "Sharing in Christ's Ministry" Consultation, on 14-19 November, to which 40 came. There were also 2-3 day Consultations in various parts of the Country with the President's Council, the Methodist Divisional Boards, Meth Soc Presidents and Secretaries, the National Children's Home General Committee, University Chaplains, Service Chaplains, and the Methodist Association of Youth Clubs.

The Media are often condemned for their lack of interest in, or their misrepresentation of Christian leaders. My experience was the opposite. In many TV and Radio interviews, in long articles in the popular press, I was faithfully represented, taken seriously, and encouraged to develop what I wanted to say. If anything, it was the religious press which failed to follow up matters which had plainly become of national interest - as; indeed, they were concerned with national issues. One BBC Radio 4 "Week Ending" Friday at 11pm programme was a skit on Thatcher, Vincent, and the country's needs.

PRESIDENTIAL AFTERMATH

As Edward Rogers once said "When you are President, you are It. When you are ex President, you are Ex-It!" In fact, I was as busy after my year as during it – including several appointments and tasks postponed from my year. But other issues became the preoccupations of the denomination, and what I had sought to make priorities were edged out. I have continued to attend Conference for at least the first day, every June/July. But it is always a mixed bag. From 1990 to 2005, with Leslie Griffiths, I maintained the Conference Open Air Meeting, continuing a Donald Soper tradition, with himself as part of it until his last appearance with myself at Tower Hill in London in the year of his death in 1997.

In 1993, we took a Petition of Distress from the Cities to London, and appealed for a Royal Commission on the cities, but had to settle for a Commission of our own, which took *The Cities: A Methodist Report* to Parliament in 1997. What else happened in Methodism, at least in my view since then, is in the 2015 book *Methodism Unbound: Christ and Methodism for the 21st Century*, continued in essays, edited by myself, *Methodism Abounding* (2016).

13

DIVIDED BRITAIN

Grace

At the beginning of John's year as Methodist President, I decided to write a letter to the *Methodist Recorder*, explaining why I was not free to go round the connexion with John, as other Presidents' wives had done.

In the letter, published on 14th September 1989, I wrote as follows.

THE "OTHER" METHODISM

"When I have gone with John to some event in the "other" Methodism – I mean to comfortable, well-peopled, generous, warm and friendly congregations, in attractive, well maintained, and unvandalised buildings – I have been repeatedly disturbed by the profound difference between these two worlds, and our ultimate inability to convey the reality of inner city life to our suburban friends. At least not enough to make any difference! I thought I would make another attempt.

"It's permanently 'backs to the wall' in the inner city. So out of desperation, new ideas and experiments have taken root. The little congregation to which I belong, Grimesthorpe Methodist Church, works from a tiny corner shop premises in the narrow streets by the dead steelworks; a vastly more appropriate location, with the shop windows to see what's happening and a totally unchurchy look, than the huge Wesley Hall it was forced to vacate nine years ago. From here, we run an old people's lunch club, a youth club, a youth club and an English class for the Asian women living around. A dozen of us worship in a participatory and human way in a circle in our back room chapel (which used to be an off-licence!) while children peer in the window at the sound of our lusty singing. Most of the members are in their 80s and 90s and get there in our car.

"There is a sense of isolation, neglect almost, by the rest of the world and Methodism. We perhaps share a sense of voicelessness and powerlessness that the poor people of our nation feel. The more we shout, the less we seem to be heard. It is against heavy odds that people find their way here to live and work and/or study at the Urban Theology Unit or in the Inner City Ecumenical Mission.

"My hope is that John's Presidency will bring the work and need of our inner city and housing estate people all over Britain to the serious attention of Methodism, both in terms of finance and personnel. Perhaps there will be more Methodists, young and not so young, who will hear the call to give some time and commitment to them. This year or next."

INNER CITY FUND

I received 96 very thoughtful letters in response, all but three favourable. I was not asking for money at all, merely describing our situation, but I had an outpouring of generosity – cheques from £5 to £500 totalling £5,500. This went in to John's Inner City Fund, which he got money for during the year of his Presidency. This gave us a total of £30,000 which we used for various inner city projects. The final £9000 helped Ashram buy 86 Spital Hill.

But I have to say that now nothing has changed. The Two Methodisms are still wide apart. The "massive conversion of comfortable Methodism" hoped for did not happen.

In 2017, it seems even further away.

14

POLITICS

John

Obviously, politics is not my prime concern. But to try to serve the Gospel in the real world means that you have to play it out on the political scene, at least on specific issues. In this chapter, I relate some political engagements and the wider thinking they represented and provoked.

CND

In 1957, I had written some letters in the *Guardian* concerning nuclear weapons. The editor Alistair Hetherington met with Donald Pennington of Manchester University, and myself on the invitation of Lord Simon of Wythenshawe for a meeting in his home in Didsbury. We decided to form a North West Campaign for Nuclear Disarmament .We held open-air meetings and marches, and opened an office in Tib Street, Manchester. Grace joined the campaign soon after we met in February 1958. She chose *Sanity* as the title for the Newsletter – later adopted by CND nationally.

My case in *Christ in a Nuclear World* (1962) was that nuclear weapons constituted both a new issue beyond pacifism, and also that Christianity was essentially a "unilateral initiative" that facilitated human problem resolution. *Christian Nuclear Perspective* (1964) argued that the whole purpose of Christianity was to show a "Way" whereby worldly and political tragedies could be dealt with by creating a "breakthrough" on the part of one-party, a "unilateral initiative" which would create a new situation to which the other side would be drawn to respond.

As CND became a very large organisation, I found it impossible to spend as much time on it. I have always found it difficult to deal with national issues, pressures and responsibility, while at the same time seeking to develop new avenues and structures for a regenerated and more credible grass-roots Christianity. On a couple of occasions, Bruce Kent and I have discussed just this issue – with mutual respect for the different ways we chose.

For the record, I was also a founding member of the New Economics Foundation (1975) and of Charter 88 (1988), but again found the meetings in London to be totally impossible in the context of all my other commitments.

CHRISTIAN SOCIALISM

In 1993, Tony Blair wrote a preface to Chris Bryant's collection of recent Tawney lectures – those of Paul Boateng (1990), myself (1991), Bob Holman (1992), and John Smith (1993), plus chapters by Hilary Armstrong and Chris Smith. The book was titled *Reclaiming the Ground*. My contribution was on "Jesus as Politician", and detailed the Project, the Strategy and the Practice of Jesus in relation to the political realities of his time, as a model for how we might act politically today. This I called "the commanding heights" of a proposed Christian politics.

But I also tried to relate to the political realities in *Britain in the 90's*: where I say the following:

"Yet to attempt Christian politics in the 90s means that we have to start rebuilding the foundations of Christian political thought and action almost from nothing. I am not competent to do this in the sphere of political theory, let alone party politics. I have lived through decades in which the great slogans of the political Left have been taken over by the other side. Freedom has become freedom of opportunity. Equality has become equality in being able to acquire as much as we like. Democracy means winning over as many as we can, believing their private interests will be best served by the party". (p. 68)

Little did I know that precisely these new definitions of the Left's slogans would become the rallying cries of New Labour, a few years later!

In 2011, Christian Socialist Movement, became "Christians on the Left", which seems to me yet another move in precisely the wrong direction! I withdrew my membership. In 2017, it's hard to know what to say!

HOUSE OF COMMONS

I became an occasional Speaker in House of Commons events around Reports or campaigns in which I was involved. I gave four lectures during my Methodist Presidential Year (1989-90), plus the launch of *The Cities* Report, (1997) and the launch of the Columbia Civil Rights Delegation (1993) Report, *Por La Vida* (1994).

One oddity typifies my engagement with politics and also my incompetence with political realities. In 1997, after the launch for The Methodist Report on *The Cities* in the House of Commons, Lord Archer- Peter Archer, an old OCW contemporary, led me into the House of Lords and asked "How would you like to be in here? We need you here". For a few months, the question was debated. Donald Soper was highly sceptical, and sought a more appropriate Methodist for the House of Lords in Kathleen Richardson, appointed in 1998. I am bound to say that I had never been attracted to frequent trips to London, and had never had any patience with assemblies of talk. So it was a merciful deliverance. And my colleague Kathleen Richardson, followed in 2001 by Leslie Griffiths, have been far, far better Lord/Ladyships than I would ever have been.

David Blunkett was not involved in all this. His visits with us were as old friends, not political planners. In 2006, David brought round to us his book, *The Blunkett Tapes*, subtitled *"My Life in the Bear Pit"*! I had enough bear pits already!

STUDENT CHRISTIAN MOVEMENT

Largely through speaking at SCM Conferences and doing University Missions, I became convinced that we needed to have residential inner city communities for training young people in Discipleship and Ministry. In the1970's, SCM's Viv Broughton set up SCM Houses, then Wick Court in Bristol, and we in Ashram Community had five inner city Community Houses. In 1972, we started our first UTU Study Year, based on studies of New Testament, Theology, History, Economics and Social Action, Urban Studies, and Community Development.

For SCM, I contributed to various volumes, like *No More Mr Nice Guy* (1991), *Introducing Christianity* (2003), *Just Visions* (2004), *Post Christianity* (2006) and *Reading the Bible* (2007) and then in the Joint Ashram–SCM "Pocket Radical" on *Discipleship* (2007). My joint book with Morna Hooker, *The Drama of Mark* (2010) began as talks at the 2007 SCM Conference. SCM brought a work camp to Burngreave Ashram, 2005-6-7.

COMMUNITY PROJECTS

Community Projects are to me the logical implication of joining in Jesus-style community development – the theory of which, and some instances, is in *Radical Jesus*, and *Christ in the City*, while Sheffield inner city experiments, are in *Into the City* and *Hope from the City*.

Three time consuming and very bottom-up examples indicate how, once you are into this "incarnational societal/community ministry" in one project, it takes you over for some years.

1. Pitsmoor Action Group, 1970-80. City councillors and friends from all three parties were co-chairs – David Blunkett for Labour, Francis Butler for Liberals, plus David Chapman for Conservatives. We formed ten Neighbourhood Groups, foxed a local demolition scheme, produced our own Neighbourhood Plan – *Pitsmoor for Tomorrow*(1978), and developed "Alternative Planning" with the then S. Yorks County Council (1975-76) with a report *South Yorkshire in Search of a Soul* (1976). Mike Newton was instigator and colleague in all this.

2. Sheffield Churches Community Programme, 1981-86. This was a self-run local Community Programme Agency based in local churches, as part of the Government's Manpower Services Commission, with Ian Lucraft, Margaret Mackley and Ian McCollough as key colleagues . At its height, we had 160 unemployed people in local projects. There are disadvantages as well as advantages to such schemes, as is clear in our 2000 Report (in *Christ in the City*, pp. 130-131).

3. Burngreave New Deal Partnership Board, 2001-11. We had £52 million to spend, as we were one of the 32 most deprived areas in Britain. We made a "Working Together" agreement with Sheffield City Council, but we had to demonstrate "additionality" through our

own extra money. We spent too much on buildings, though Sorby House, Forum House and Vestry Hall are now useful assets.

By 2010, the only continuing Partnership Board members from the 25 elected were four ex- UTU Study Year companions – Beryl Peck, Chris Sissons, Jean Wildgoose, and myself. "Well we said it was long-term commitment", we joked.

In the midst of this, in 2007-08, I had the honour to be Lord Mayor's Chaplain for our Burngreave Ward Councillor and long-time friend Jackie Drayton. With David Blunkett's involvement, we had some significant Town Hall occasions, not least one on Regeneration, for which I produced a Report (in *Christ in the City*, pp. 130-131).

I was also a Trustee of Emmaus Sheffield from 1990 to 2015. It now has a community of 19 residential companions operating a Furniture Rehab and Shop, from down in the Sheffield Canal Basin.

MEDIA

Throughout the 1960's and 70's, I was often engaged in Sunday morning religious programmes on BBC Radio and on BBC TV, especially for producers RT Brooks and Roger Hutchings. Alan Dale and myself wrote and presented two series of programmes on themes of the Gospels in 1971-72. Other TV programmes were in "Seeing and Believing" in January and May 1969, January 1974, and February and July 1977.

Once one becomes a familiar face and voice, TV can easily become an assumed medium. On the first day of Arthur Scargill's Orgreave Colliery Strike in June 1984, a BBC Pantechnicon arrived outside 239 Abbeyfield Road, asking for an interview. "Sorry", I replied "I am not the right person. Go up to Barnsley and find the Industrial Chaplain". They did.

During the Methodist Presidential Year and after, Radio 4 Sunday Programme brought me regularly into Radio Sheffield to comment on this and that – usually political matters, and on several occasions took me for an overnight in a Piccadilly hotel to be live in the Oxford Road studios at Manchester, and finally to a 20th year "Sunday" programme Celebration event in 2001.

In June 2000, I was in London TV Centre for a half-hour programme on the "Soul of Britain", concerned with "Consumerism". Another speaker and I battled hard to present a critical and prophetic view. At the end, I confessed to the producer, David Coombes that I felt that we had failed. He comforted me with the words "There is no place on Television for Alternatives". In the twelve months that followed, I was telephoned by an assistant to quiz me as to whether my views would be useful for specific "Moral Maze" programmes, on three occasions. Each time, I obviously failed to say what they wanted me to say! I listen with admiration and incredulity to my friends Alan Billings and Leslie Griffiths, maintaining the brilliant tradition of Donald Soper and Colin Morris in commenting on issues. But I don't seem to have "opinions" on things, and certainly have neither time nor mind for endless talk not based on practice or usefulness. Which makes me a rather dull, single line, incommunicative' media non-personality! I'm no good at "small talk" anyway – as friends observe.

Mainly when Walter Schwarz, an MGS History Sixth friend, was Religious Correspondent for *The Guardian*, I did a dozen *"Face to Faith"* articles (1980-1994), and occasional articles at other times.

I am not sure that much media does more good than harm. Occasionally, you should avoid it. On returning after the South Africa visit in 1978, I decided to do no press conferences or articles, for fear of endangering the many black church leaders who had accompanied us and worked with us, in violation, they said of the Apartheid laws. Whilst there, we and our escorts got arrested in the Regina Mundi Cathedral at Soweto, and our experience in the Soweto Police station left us determined not to give any "leads" to the Afrikaaner police.

I don't believe that "discretion is the better part of valour". But I do conclude that much harm is done by much speaking, rather than much acting, with a sentence or two before and after. But that would be too "alternative", particularly were it – as mine would be - theologically motivated.

Totally unrelated to the vagaries of immediate politics, David Blunkett has been our guest at home almost every year for forty five years. This has been for us an inspiring and faithful friendship, which happily still continues today.

JESUS AND POLITICS

In all these instances, half of the question in my mind is the impossible one - What Would Jesus Do? (WWJD).

It has brought the Inner City Missioner and the New Testament Theologian into endless debate. Even now, 2017, I am trying to see wood for trees, in a book called *Jesus and Politics*. At least, I think I know the answer to – What Did Jesus Do?

Reference.

David Blunkett, *The Blunkett Tapes: My Life in the Bear Pit*. London: Bloomsbury 2006.

15

FAMILY

Grace

How do a wife and family fit into the crazy life we've had?

For a start, we would have to say that while John and I had a shared ministry, he is mainly the head and I am mainly the hands.

Equally, in the lives of family and children, we have been parents together, but the main responsibility for home and children has been mine, if only because John's ministerial work took him out of the house most evenings and many weekends, quite apart from wider travel inside and outside England as his activities and influence developed.

CHRIS, FAITH AND JAMES

Our children's lives have been lived like ours, in inner city areas. Since we came to Sheffield in 1970, Burngreave – Pitsmoor has become very multi-cultural. Firshill Primary School where they attended is now almost totally non-white. There have been many drug related issues and frequent violence outside our Burngreave Ashram building. We have even had a murder on the side street. But I won't exaggerate the difficulties, for it has also been enriching if very demanding. And things are much better now in 2017.

We sent our children, Chris, Faith and James to local schools as a matter of principle, not thinking it right to give our children a more privileged education than the children living locally received. They all went to Firshill Primary School, across the road and then to Firth Park Secondary. Sadly, this proved a serious mistake as the schools were not adequate or educationally challenging. They all felt it had been wrong and very unfair. John and I were deceived on two counts – first, the false claim that Firth Park continued its old Grammar School standards; second, the nonsense that home rather than school contributes most to a child's development. Over supper at home with us in 1997, David Blunkett, who had just become Secretary of State for Education, declared that he had three of the worst schools in England in his constituency – one of them being Firth Park.

Chris finished his A levels at Firth Park and went to Manchester University to take a B.A. in History and Politics. Then he spent a year doing a PGCE in Sheffield and a further year at Leeds doing an MA in Politics, with a Thesis on Thatcherism. From 1994 to 2012 he taught at Norton and Hillsborough campuses of Sheffield College. Since 2012 he has studied at Hallam University in media and film, and developed Virtual Education, a project for tutoring online.

Chris settled in Sheffield with Carol and they had two children – Reuben in 1989 and Cecelia in 1996. They live down the road from where we live. Chris was also Secretary to the Burngreave Ward Labour Party with Councillor Howard Knight.

Faith attended at Firth Park and then went to Manchester to study Art, where she met Tony. The two of them went for further study, Faith at Brighton and Tony at Chelsea, for a Fine Arts Degree, and then both for an MA at the Slade, in University College, London. In 1989 – 90, Faith had a Wingate Scholarship to study Fresco painting in Prato in Italy. John and I visited her for Christmas 1989, after which we went down to Rome, to the English College and had an audience with the Pope, during John's Presidential year.

Faith and Tony had two children, Iona born in 1992 and Honor in 1996. The family home is in Highbury, with a studio together in Finsbury Park, from where they work and exhibit their work. Both lecture at the City Lit Covent Garden.

James followed the others to Firth Park up to O level. We wrote a letter of protest to the school governors, and James at Faith's insistence was moved to Tapton School across the city, from there followed a place at the London School of Economics. Whilst there, he did voluntary work in Richard Caborn's office in the House of Commons.

James ended up in Venice Beach, Los Angeles, where he set up the Media Arts Lab, doing world-wide advertising for Apple

75

Computers. He figures frequently in Walter Isaacson's book *Steve Jobs*. More recently he has created a new company, FNDR, advising Founders of companies such as AirBnB. James married Marie in Belgium and they have two children, Leo (2005) and Manon (2008).

FAMILY AND MINISTRY

Can family and ministry go together?

Family and ministry had to fit in together somehow. An example from the children's teenage years shows how we tried to keep together family life. John's ministry was extending all the time, especially with lecture tours, and setting up transatlantic urban ministry courses in the USA. The family joined him on two occasions, visiting and staying with friends. There is an old tradition in Methodism of helping ministers, who are not well paid. So from 1960 to 1975, we had free holidays in homes of other ministers or well-wishers in various parts of the country.

An example is in 1978, John had two periods in the USA. Then in July we had a family holiday at John's mother's caravan at Grindleford. In August we two spent three weeks in South Africa, lecturing and visiting in Johannesburg, Capetown, Grahamstown, Soweto, and Pietermaritzburg. This included amazing and memorable private visits to Beyers Naude, Desmond Tutu and Alex Borraine. Then in early October John was in Boston, Newark, Drew and New York, conducting or arranging UTUNA Transatlantic Urban Ministry courses. But then for October half term, the family had a week again at Kirkmoor, near Robin Hood's Bay, with John calling in to speak to the Leeds University Anglican/Methodist Society at 4pm and being back for a SICEM service, at 6.30pm at Pitsmoor.

Weekends always had to be carefully planned, with John visiting yearly 8 or more Universities, SCMs and Meth Socs, besides hosting four "Come Down Our Street Lord" weekends in Sheffield for "enquirers". Ten to fifteen came for each UTU Study Year partly from these weekends. But weekends were not family occasions, with Saturdays being used for conferences, and Sundays for conducting services. Ashram weekends and holidays were family events, to which we all went together, and to which we later took grandchildren.

When John went away to visit a University he sometimes would take one of the children, especially James. When in 1979-83 he did summers at Drew in USA he took Chris one year, and Faith went with him one year to stay with Neil and Ila Fisher in Evanston.

JOINT MINISTRY

And so, looking back, our life has been richly satisfying and rewarding, if full of struggles and challenges. It has been a joint ministry. To say John is the head and I am the hands is not strictly true, for John set up many practical projects. But in the everyday, it has been I who have sorted things for the family, and dealt with issues in our projects. I have thrived on such practicalities. The system between us has worked well. We automatically support what the other has done or said – for good or ill! In June 2014, I did a talk on "Creating Gospel Projects" for the St. Mark's Broomhill Centre for Radical Christianity, of which John was with Marcus Borg a Patron. "We want you, not John" they said. We did the evening together! And every Sunday morning, John is preaching all around Sheffield. We go together – and test out local pub lunches together afterwards!

In July 1991, we moved out of the Methodist manse at 239 Abbeyfield Road, and into a smaller 1930's semi nearby, at 178 Abbeyfield Road. In 2016, we found a smaller semi at 7 College Court, just round the corner. Our Chris and Carol are still nearby, and their son Reuben has a Sheffield base in our back bedroom.

Reference
Walter Issacson, *Steve Jobs*. London: Little, Brown, 2011

THE YEAR 2017

But now...

On 27-29 April, we spent three days in Highbury with Faith and her family. Then on 30 April, New Roots had a party (and a brilliant speech by John) on its 30th Anniversary. May 5-7 brought Ashram members for their bi-annual weekend at Middleton, from where we all plus visitors, had a 50th Anniversary Celebration at Champness Hall, Rochdale, with several old members and Community House residents.

I had had an Endoscopy on 22 March which showed some stomach inflammation, and had a CT Scan. On 9 May, our very caring doctor Clare Richardson spent an hour with us. I have cancer of the pancreas and liver and face an uncertain future. My increasingly painful condition affects what I can do.

I am continuing with John at things as I can, with family and friends around or coming to visit.

Our planned Vincent family Reunion on 29 July, for which we hoped to have copies of this book, is postponed.

So my part of our rich and wonderful life draws to a close.

17 May 2017.

Died 25 May 2017

16

CHANGING THE WORLD

John

GREATER THAN OURSELVES

So, what is to be said at the end? What on earth did we think we were doing?

It is all about personal passions, we think – and practical projects. But the key is the personal passion. And for us the personal passions had a theological origin.

We got landed in Sheffield as a result of some classic mistakes by myself in sorting out our projects. But we stayed because it suited our passions.

Our passions derived from what I discovered about a method historically originating in Jesus. I had become convinced that Christianity had to start all over again, at the bottom of society. We knew, as educated middle class people, that it would never be a complete incarnation there for us. But our passion was to try to live out some of the fundamental ideas and practices of Jesus, which would always inevitably be somewhat troublesome.

So we stayed, and made many mistakes. Our children suffered through poor local schools. We lost some of our culture. We were perhaps brought down to size.

Reflecting this, our daughter Faith at the Celebration for Grace on 4th June declared:

Grace's don't come around very often, and we feel privileged to have been part of that momentum. Life was not always easy, but it was never dull, and we always felt part of something that was greater than ourselves.

So, what is the "Something greater than ourselves"? It was fundamentally about changing the world.

CHANGING THE WORLD

Grace and I saw ourselves not primarily as representatives of religion, or Methodism, or Christianity as a religion. Rather, our concentration was upon an ever fruitful and ever revealing attempt to carry out our joint ministry as contemporary followers of Jesus. As I said at the Celebration, Grace was not a God person, and was highly sceptical of all forms of religion. But she was a Jesus person. She regarded everyone as potential and actual significant actors in human life, as interpreted by Jesus. She often quoted Dorothea Sölle's "Song on the Road to Emmaus", which ends,

> We are the water of life
> We shall find the water
> We shall be the water

As our son James put it afterwards, it's about doing it not saying it. Jesus did it and was it by the decisions he made, so we did it because we were intentional disciples of his, carrying on his celebration of the Kingdom of God / heaven present on earth.

This puts us, we think, not among the great thinkers, religious leaders, philosophers or theologians. But it puts us with Ghandi – "Be the change you want to see in the world". Or with Ernst Schmacher – "Small is Beautiful". Or Mother Teresa who when asked "How are you going to save all the children in the world?" replied "One by one". And with David Blunkett, who hailed us as showing "the crucial role of those whose Faith drives them to give their lives to others." Or with Donald Soper: "John Vincent is a *devôt*, and we need more like him for the work of the Lord and the wellbeing of God's world".

Can you change the world from the bottom? That is perhaps still the question. But we cannot wait for an answer. We have to get on with whatever bits we can answer. We have to get on with whatever bits we can manage, in the attempt. We have to take "unilateral initiatives", as Jesus did.

80

A PATTERN OF LIFE

Thus, the two of us endlessly reflected on what this meant in practice. In Chapter 8 I outline a "Gospel Pattern" based on the life and practice of Jesus, which I then use as a series of models for our inner city ministry work.

However, the Jesus based Pattern was originally used not for Projects but as a way of describing what a Jesus – based personal philosophy and behaviour might look like. In *The Jesus Thing* (1973),p.60, I indicate personal ways of ourselves imitating the successive elements in the Way of Jesus, the Dynamics of Christ.

- Getting where people are, living with them, sharing their lot. (Incarnation)

- Ministering to people's real need, alongside the poor, washing feet, cleaning streets. (Healing)

- Lifting up points, people, groups, happenings, that bring love, acceptance, significance. (Parables)

- Small, strategic actions, which are prophetic signs, imaginative instances, of new possibilities. (Acted Parables)

- Groups of people with a discipline and a corporate commitment to acting together, (Disciple Groups)

- Polarization, conflict, as powers and people in power are exposed, and fight back. (Crucifixion)

- Reversals, in which the new deed catches on, the new style evokes response. (Resurrection)

- Bits of success within history, even the triumph of the new Way. (New Jerusalem)

Each of these elements have been manifest at different stages in our story, and provide for us the secret inner narrative for it.

CHANGING WHAT YOU CAN

Behind these efforts were two convictions. First, we were convinced, negatively, that current and conventional ways were damaging to the essential Way of Jesus. Second, we were convinced that you had to create alternatives.

Suburban Christianity warped it to suit the rich. You needed a distinctive and new approach in the inner city – SICEM. Universities and Religious Denominations translated Christianity into forms to suit themselves. You needed a context at the bottom of society, like where Jesus worked – UTU. Majority and institutional opinions would never support radical change. So you needed a community to nurture it – Ashram. And academic and theoretical theology had not led to discipleship-centred, world–changing Christianity. You had to work at a new theology – Radical Christianity. (We're both in a 2016 publication with this title).

Our Intentional Communities were to serve these fundamental reversals. The alliance of small inner city churches was to protect them from the suburbs – SICEM. Our Seminary of the Street, based in inner city houses, provided a new context for encountering a contemporary Christ – UTU. Our Community of fellow radicals developed inner city community houses - Ashram. And we campaigned for and wrote of a New Theology – Radical Christianity.

These small efforts, painful, time consuming, controversy creating and inevitably fragile, were themselves ways to get at the fundamental life and world changing practice of Jesus and some of the first Christians. What I called "Journey Downwards" was the initial implication for those not "incarnates", to get themselves into the dynamic. And, since whatever you did was not the complete change that was needed, it was only but significantly an "Acted Parable" for that change. And, since what you were doing, was always counter what was there already, you needed "Unilateral Initiative" to get the movement, then a "Disciple Group" of Intentional Community to continue it. These use the Jesus-style tactics and structures for "Changing the World from the bottom".

Preoccupied with these theologically motivated, counter-cultural models, it was more easy to ignore or avoid possibilities which might have been advantageous to us, but which just did not fit our model of changing the world from the bottom. Which I suppose explains the many dead-ends in our story - "Ways Not Travelled".

But, as I have always said - Go for what is going for you, not for what is not going for you! Get Heaven on earth going for you, and go for your bit towards it!

Globalise it, and we're changing the world.

CELEBRATION OF GRACE

There were beautiful recollections of Grace at the Celebration and Thanksgiving, with 150 people filling Pitsmoor Methodist Church, conducted by Ian Lucraft on 3rd June 2017. Frederick Stafford spoke on India and Ulster, Faith and James on Family in Sheffield, Andrew Weeks on New Roots and Ashram Community, and grandson Reuben on Life at 178 Abbeyfield Road. Lord David Blunkett sent a tribute, Councillor Jackie Drayton spoke on Pitsmoor and Burngreave Community, and I spoke on Celebrating Grace's Life and Ministry, printed in *ACT Together*, Autumn 2017. Lovely obituaries were published in the *Sheffield Star*, the *Sheffield Telegraph*, and the *Methodist Recorder* (Andrew Weeks), each on the 22nd June, in *The Guardian* (Alice McGregor) on 11th July, and in the *Burngreave Messenger* (Cecelia Vincent) in July.

References
Dorothea Sölle "Song on the Road to Emmaus",
Revolutionary Patience, London: Lutterwoth Press, 1979, pp.22-24, p.24

David Blunkett, Foreword to John Vincent, *Hope from the City*
Peterborough: Epworth Press, 2000. p. xi

Donald Soper. Preface to John Vincent, *Discipleship in the 90s*, Peterborough: Methodist Publishing House 1991, p.1.

John Vincent "Jesus the Radical",
Grace Vincent "Radical Christianity in Gospel Projects",
in *Radical Christianity: Roots and Fruits*, ed. Chris Rowland and John Vincent, Sheffield, Urban Theology Unit . 2016

Grace Vincent – A life of sharing

Grace was an inspirational woman, she was kind and generous. She combined family, work and community with giving something back and making a difference – and of course – with changing the world!

Whatever Grace took on she put her heart and soul into it. As a teacher in both Burngreave Middle School and Earl Marshal Secondary School her hard work, dedication and love of learning, as well as her expectations and respect for her pupils and their families – ensured that aspirations were raised and they strived to achieve their full potential.

This love of learning – sharing, discussions and debating ideas with others – continued throughout her life and into her work in the community. Whether working in the New Roots for Justice shop, Burngreave Ashram or the UTU or on the many new ideas and projects she was involved in. Whatever needed to be done was shared – Grace would do her share – and more! – cleaning, serving, cleaning rubbish or cooking – giving help, support, encouragement or listening to all those in need. Grace was there – always with one of her cakes on hand to be shared.

Grace was a remarkable woman with an incisive and independent mind, loyal, loving and compassionate with immense energy.

Grace's 'joy of sharing' touched many – it influenced and made 'life changing' impressions on many people including me!

She will be missed by many but I know her legacy will live on.

    Jackie Drayton

Grace Vincent obituary

Alice McGregor

Thursday 6 July 2017 16.10 BST

My friend and colleague Grace Vincent, who has died aged 83, was committed to the cause of social justice, and her example inspired many others.

With her husband, John, a Methodist minister, Grace founded the Ashram Community in Rochdale, Greater Manchester, in 1967. They were part of a movement that asserted the importance of following the radical example of Jesus in living a Christian life, with the aim of making a significant difference in the world. The community adopted both the eastern concept of building a spiritual resource and the western emphasis on commitment to working among people experiencing poverty.

Grace and John encompassed the very best of modern Christianity, combining vision with day-to-day application. This always took a bottom-up approach, working with people rather than on their behalf, both in community work and in style of worship. Through the Ashram Community, Grace provided support and encouragement to several generations of people living in disadvantaged urban areas.

Grace was born in Kodaikanal, south India, daughter of the Rev Wilfred Stafford and his wife, Dora (nee Johnston), Irish Methodist missionaries. The family remained in India until Grace was 14, when she was sent to school at Methodist college, Belfast. She later studied English literature at Queen's University Belfast and in 1958 married John Vincent.

From the Rochdale mission, Grace and John moved in 1970 to inner-city Sheffield, where Grace taught English as a second language at local schools. She set up New Roots, a wholefoods "shop for justice" that inspired many, including me and other local students, with its evident call to environmental and social justice.

This stands alongside the inner-city work the Ashram Community established and still sustains, most notably at the Burngreave Ashram in Sheffield, which offers a weekly free meal to all (Grace last took part a week before her death) and where destitute migrants and homeless people are often housed. There are also a number of community houses in the area and those living in them work and volunteer locally. The Ashram Community has spread throughout the UK and continues to be inspired and guided by Grace and John's vision, writings and dedication.

John and their three children, Christopher, Faith and James, survive her.

17

YET ALIVE

John

YET ALIVE!

So what remains?

I hesitate to predict the future. Karl Barth I heard several times announcing plans for future writings, adding "Wenn wir noch leben" – If we are yet alive. I recall this when each year the former Methodist Presidents, including myself, assemble with the whole Annual Conference, and sing with gusto:

> And are we yet alive
>
> And see each other's face?

I always have to bear in mind that my mother lived to her 110th year. And I add to that the fact that Methodist ministers normally nowadays live into their nineties. Of the 25 of us who started at Richmond College in 1951, a good two thirds are still alive, and only a few of those who came to our 50th year Reunion in 2001 are not here, still.

I am still active enough. I have restarted my daily morning jogging rather than an afternoon walk, initially with Grace – but still in nearby Burngreave Cemetery, our local countryside. In October 2017, I go with grandson Reuben to New York, with Geoff Curtiss and Don Rudalevige, for a UTUNA and UMTP Reunion, and to spend time at our James's new Brooklyn apartment.

UNFINISHED BUSINESS

I've always tried to write books *after* there were happenings demanding them. The present volume puts my theological and literary works over the decades into the circumstances and contexts from within which and often for which they were written. But, if we are yet alive, there are several projects, which I hope will appear in the next few years, which continue trajectories discernible here, on which I am currently working.

- Discipleship in the New Testament. Essays by Anglicans and Methodists on this new emphasis. (Edited)

- Outworkings. Mark 1-6 in Personal Practice Interpretation

- Discipleship in Mark. A radical re-writing of the 1975 edition of my doctorate

- Jesus and Politics. A commissioned volume in the Biblical Challenges in the Contemporary World Series

- Intentional Community. Practice Interpretation series studies of communities on the model of Jesus's Community. (Edited)

- Urban Theology Unit, 1969-2019. A Historical Record for the Jubilee, including UTUNA and UMTP.

Titles are provisional. And other things may intervene.
But sometime a Radical Dogmatics? And a Theological Autobiography?

And a real breakthrough – *Changing the World?*

RECENT BOOKS

Jesus,Gospel Studies,Discipleship.

Radical Jesus – The Way of Jesus, Then and Now. 3rd Edition. Sheffield: Ashram Press, 2015. £8.50

Radical Christianity: Roots and Fruits. Edited by Chris Rowland & John Vincent. Sheffield: Urban Theology Unit, 2016. £8.50

Urban, Liberation, Contextual Theology.

Christ in the City: The Dynamics of Christ in Urban Theological Practice. Sheffield: Urban Theology Unit, 2013. Includes Bibliography. £12.50

Methodism, Alternative Church

Methodism Unbound: Christ and Methodism for the 21st Century: Chadderton: Church in the Market Place Publications, 2015 £9.99

Ashram, Intentional Community.

A Lifestyle of Sharing: Sheffield: Ashram Press, 2009. £10

For other publications, in the four areas named, see the Bibliographies in the books.
      Send Orders with Cheque to:
      (add £1.50 for p&p)
Ashram Press, 7 College Court, Sheffield, S4 7FN
Church in the Market Place Publications, Urban Theology Unit, Victoria Hall, Norfolk Street, Sheffield, S1 2JB.

OTHER BOOKS

Other books related to our story are listed below.

Wilfred and Dora Stafford, edited by Grace Vincent. Sheffield: 1999

The Memoirs of Ethel Beatrice Vincent, 1891-2000. Edited by John Vincent, Designed by Faith Vincent. Sheffield: Crux Press, 2008

New Roots. Shop for Justice, by Grace Vincent, Third Edition. Sheffield: Ashram Press, 2015

Urban Christ: Responses to John Vincent, edited by Ian K. Duffield, Sheffield: Urban Theology Unit, 1997.
Includes complete Bibliography up to 1997.

JOHN VINCENT
A BIBLIOGRAPHY

Jesus and Discipleship

Secular Christ	Lutterworth Press/Abingdon Press, 1968
Disciple and Lord	Academy Press, 1976
Radical Jesus	Marshall Pickering, 1986
Mark at Work (Jt)	Bible Reading Fellowship, 1986
Discipleship in the 90's	Methodist Publishing House, 1991
Liberation Spirituality (Jt Ed)	Urban Theology Unit, 1999
Mark: Gospel of Action (Ed)	SPCK, 2006
Discipleship	Pocket Radicals: Ashram Press 2007
The Drama of Mark (Jt)	Epworth Press, 2010
Stilling the Storm (Ed)	Deo Publishing, 2011
The Farewell Discources in Rractice (Ed)	Deo Publishing, 2015
The Servant of God in Practice (Jt Ed)	Deo Publishing, 2016
Radical Jesus	Ashram Press, 2016

Urban Mission and Politics

Christ in a Nuclear World	Crux Press, 1962
The Race Race	SCM Press / Friendship Press, 1969
Starting All Over Again	WCC Risk Books, 1981
Into the City	Epworth Press, 1982
Britain in the 90's	Methodist Publishing House, 1989
The Cities: A Methodist Report (Jt Ch)	NCH Action for Children, 1997
Gospel from the City (Jt Ed)	Urban Theology Unit, 1997
Hope from the City	Epworth Press, 2000
Faithfulness in the City (Ed)	Monad Press, 2003
The City in Biblical Perspective (Jt)	Equinox, 2009
Christ in the City	Urban Theology Unit, 2013
For Church and Nation (Jt Ed)	Urban Theology Unit, 2013

Theology & Church

Christ and Methodism	Epworth Press / Abingdon Press, 1965
Here I Stand	Epworth Press, 1967
The Jesus Thing	Epworth Press / Abingdon Press, 1973
Alternative Church	Christian Journals, 1976
Stirrings: Essays Christian & Radical (Ed)	Epworth Press, 1976
OK, Let's Be Methodists	Epworth Press, 1984
Gospel in the 90's	Methodist Publishing House, 1990
Liberation Theology UK (Jt Ed)	Urban Theology Unit, 1995
Methodist and Radical (Jt Ed)	Abingdon Press / Alban Books, 2004
Outworkings: Gospel Practice and Interpretation	Urban Theology Unit, 2005
A Lifestyle of Sharing	Ashram Press, 2009
Christian Communities (Ed)	Ashram Press, 2011
Acts in Practice (Ed)	Deo Publishing, 2012
Methodism Unbound	Church in the Market Place. 2015
Radical Christianity: Roots and Fruits (Ed)	Urban Theology Unit, 2016
Methodism Abounding (Ed)	Church in the Market Place, 2016

89

INDEX

Single mentions in lists not included

Hale Methodist Church 16, 17, 23,
Hebden, Keith 46,
Howell, John 50-55,

Incarnation 9, 41, 44, 79, 81, 82,
Inner City 9,10, 36, 42, 47-48, 57, 65-66, 74, 82,
Intentional Community 33, 36-40, 69, 81, 82, 87, 88

Jesus 10,16, 24, 38, 43, 44, 62, 68-72, 73,79, 81, 82, 86, 87
Jones, Richard G 27, 35, 37, 61, 62
Journey Course 38
Journey Downwards 46, 62, 66, 82

Kingdom of God on Earth 10, 44, 62, 80, 81, 82

Lucraft, Ian G. 8, 43, 70

Mackley, Margaret   8, 47, 70,
MacLeod, George 26, 27, 30, 33, 37, 38
Manchester Grammar School 14-15, 17, 55
Manchester University 45
Mason, David M. 24, 26, 34, 37, 41
Media 55, 63, 71-72
Methodism 16, 37, 60-61, 63-64, 65-66, 85, 86, 88
Methodist Conference 25, 30, 39, 41-42, 60-62, 86
Methodist Recorder 8, 24, 34, 61, 65, 83
Methodist Renewal Group 27, 28
Ministry 27, 44, 52, 60, 63, 77, 81, 82
Mission Alongside the Poor 61, 81
Morris, Colin 60, 62, 72
Morton, Harry 26, 27, 41, 60
Multi Faith 46, 58

Namibia House 59
New Roots 38, 55-58, 78, 84, 85, 88
New Testament Studies 25, 26, 30, 31, 45, 46, 69, 72, 73, 82, 87, 89
New York Theological Seminary 35, 45, 76

Order of Christian Witness 21, 23, 26, 69

Parliament, Houses of 54,64, 69
Petition of Distress from the Cities 64
Pitsmoor Action Group 42, 70
Politics 10, 30, 44, 46, 61-63, 64, 67-73, 81, 87
Poor, Poverty 42, 46, 58, 61, 62, 64, 65-66, 79
Practice Interpretation 45, 46, 87
Presidency of Methodist Conference 60-64, 71, 86

Radical Christianity 34, 39, 46, 57-58, 61, 62, 77, 82, 83, 88
Richardson, Kathleen 33, 69
Richmond College 23-24, 86

Rudalevige, Don 45, 86, 87

SICEM BRANCHES

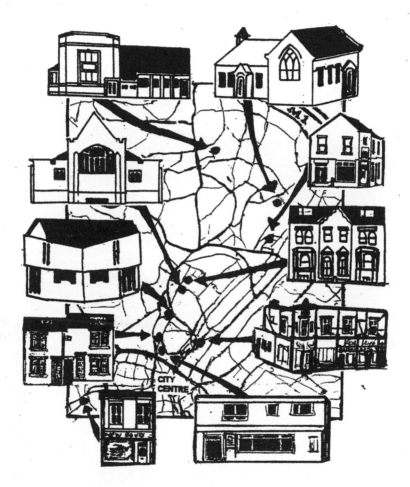

Clockwise from top left: Shiregreen United Reformed Church, Upper Wincobank Undenominational Chapel, Grimesthorpe Methodist Shop Church, Urban Theology Unit, Burngreave Ashram Shop & Centre, The Furnival, Rock Street Ashram House, New Roots Ashram Centre, Pitsmoor Methodist Church and Centre, St James United Reformed Church

WHO ARE WE?

A Community of Study, of Reflection and Prophecy, of
    Commitment and Creation,
where Christians and non-Christians, men and women, young
    and old, of all churches and none, theologians, sociologists,
    workers, ministers, housewives, teachers, social workers,
    searchers . . .

Have the chance to live and work together in inner city
    neighbourhood houses,
beside deprivation and celebration, racism and demolition . . .

Beginning at the bottom, researching issues and problems,
    taking sides with people, struggling with politics, hammering
    out new possibilities, incarnating alternatives . . .

Through studying theories and policies, reading theologies and
    scriptures,
building vocations and communities, creating models, getting
    action from theology, theology from action . . .

As a part of humanity,
in the name of Jesus Christ,
for the sake of the city,
present and future,
all over the world.[1]

Urban
Theology
Unit

210 Abbeyfield Road,
Sheffield S4 7AZ

95

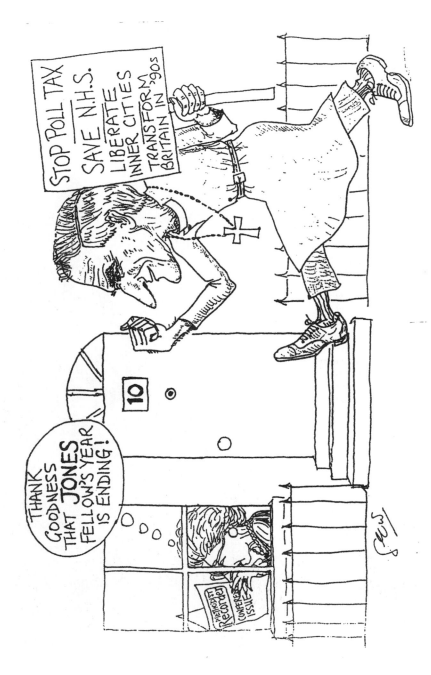

97

SHEFFIELD ASHRAM COMMUNITY

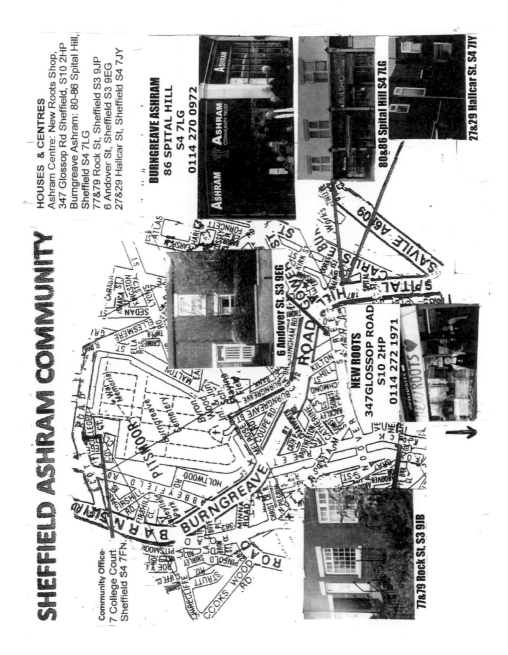

HOUSES & CENTRES

Ashram Centre: New Roots Shop,
347 Glossop Rd Sheffield, S10 2HP
Burngreave Ashram: 80-86 Spital Hill,
Sheffield S4 7LG
77&79 Rock St, Sheffield S3 9JP
6 Andover St, Sheffield S3 9EG
27&29 Hallcar St, Sheffield S4 7JY

BURNGREAVE ASHRAM
86 SPITAL HILL
S4 7LG
0114 270 0972

80&86 Spital Hill S4 7LG

27&29 Hallcar St. S4 7JY

6 Andover St. S3 9EG

NEW ROOTS
347 GLOSSOP ROAD
S10 2HP
0114 272 1971

77&79 Rock St. S3 9JB

Community Office
7 College Court
Sheffield S4 7FN.